H. W. R. (Henry W. R.) Jackson

The southern women of the second American Revolution

Their trials, etc.

H. W. R. (Henry W. R.) Jackson

The southern women of the second American Revolution
Their trials, etc.

ISBN/EAN: 9783337163365

Printed in Europe, USA, Canada, Australia, Japan

Cover: Foto ©ninafisch / pixelio.de

More available books at **www.hansebooks.com**

THE SOUTHERN WOMEN

OF THE

Second American Revolution,

THEIR TRIALS, &c.

YANKEE BARBARITY ILLUSTRATED.

OUR

NAVAL VICTORIES

AND

EXPLOITS

OF

CONFEDERATE WAR STEAMERS.

CAPTURE OF

YANKEE GUNBOATS, &c.

BY H. W. R. JACKSON.

ATLANTA, GEORGIA:
INTELLIGENCER STEAM-POWER PRESS.
1863.

PREFACE.

To whom are we indebted for our recent brilliant achievements and naval successes, but to woman. The noble action and self-sacrificing devotion of our ladies, in forwarding money and means for the construction of gunboats and battering rams wherewith to cope with an insolent and barbarian foe, is unequaled in all times past both ancient and modern. Hundreds, aye thousands, who had not the money sent forward what jewelry or silver plate they possessed as contributions. Many a birth-day present and bridal gift has been sacrificed upon the altar of liberty that urged on our men of daring to deeds of valor and renown. History does not record such unbounded and unanimously spontaneous action of a people. Did we, indeed, lack the cavalier spirit of death-daring valor in our Generals, the innate heroism, fortitude and devotion of our women would, doubtless, call forth from among their own sex a leader for our armies to forego the pleasures of ease and feminine considerations and respond to the call of temporal requirements for the occasion like a Joan of Arc.

It is but a little more than a year since our women, as with one voice, have called upon men of prominence to aid them in the construction of floating engines of war, and behold the result; it is already glorious, though, as yet, at the first breaking of the dawn of day (the day of triumph over a common enemy,) our achievements are great.

Galveston was recaptured and her blockade raised, by Gen. Magruder, with a fleet of cotton boats prepared for the purpose. He bore down upon the Federal blockading fleet, capturing four vessels, one of which the Harriet Lane, a formidable ship of war, was taken by boarding; another one of the largest was blown up with all on board, the balance having made their escape, two of which took advantage of the white flag, which was raised in token of surrender, but seeing an opportunity for escape run the gauntlet. On shore the whole Federal garrison was captured, with large quantities of stores and supplies of ammunition.

Soon after this brilliant achievement the blockade of Charleston was raised by Commodore Ingraham, who captured and sunk three of the enemies vessels. This success was followed by the gratifying results upon the Mississippi and the Cumberland Rivers, where we captured and destroyed some forty of the enemies gunboats and transports, among which were eight or nine of the most formidable gunboats and ironclads.

Since the first of January, 1863, we have captured, in serviceable condition, seven of the most formidable engines of war the enemy had afloat, which are now being turned to account in a good cause, serving in the Confederate States navy against God-defying infidelity and hell-deserving Abolitionists, who, actuated by the basest instincts of brute nature, confront us with lustful designs of fiends incarnate.

In their last and vilest of efforts, by which they attempt to incite to servile revolt our contented and happy servants, God will cause their barbarous schemes as signally to fail and miscarry as have all their former attempts at subjugation.

Let us look to our recent successes and consider well the fortitude and devotion of woman in the cause of independence and liberty from a tyranny which will soon be over, past, provided, we act with ever-increasing vigilance and determination.

Let us put our hope and trust in the God of hosts, for He hath set us apart as His chosen people, hence the scourging we are now receiving by the visitation of revolution and war which has deluged our fair land in blood and anguish. If there is a people upon the face of the earth that cannot be made slaves, but which he has appointed as his own people and agents to perpetuate the work of civilization, it is the people of the Confederate States of America, the descendants of the Caucassian and Jewish races who are entrusted with the fostering care and protection of the African race as an institution of servitude to civilization. We are commanded to foster and perpetuate this institution for the benefit of future ages. God has commanded us to buy our servants from the heathen nations to be an inheritance to our children and our children's children. The majority of our enemies, though at the commencement of the war their visions were clouded with blind philanthrophy and fanaticism, are now being informed, by the force of circumstances, by unaccustomed intercourse and association with the negro, of their error in the course and policy they have adopted with regard to the whole African race, finding they can do nothing and accomplish less with such as have been captured and others who were induced to leave their good and kind masters and mistresses, they are now being prepared, drilled and armed for service and to be placed in the front lines of battle (finding them an unwielding mass of helplessness and inferiority for the accomplishment of any other purpose.) First being placed in the front lines of battle the negro will serve as a breast work to shield the bodies and preserve the lives of degraded and polluted Yankees.

2nd. Having served such purpose and being slain upon the field of battle, the Yankees have no more trouble with Cuffee, and say he has been turned to good account.

Thus it will be seen that the poor and deluded African is to serve a two-fold purpose to the Abolition Yankee of the East, whose principles must be corrupting to the most depraved and demoniac fiends of hell.

Permit me, kind reader, to ask does not a contemplation of the Yankee character excite in you a feeling of condemnation and scorn mingled with alternate pity and contempt for our demented enemy whose every existence, *being* and *to be*, (now and forever,) is qualified by the epithet Yankee, a term comprehensibly expressive of all that is impure, inhuman, uncharitable, unchristian and uncivilized (barbarian and heathen is scarcely applicable in the case,) demons of hell in the guise of men.

I have not done yet. If, indeed, there should be a discrepancy it will be found in favor of language not containing words of sufficient force to express the baseness of the character and nature of the Yankees and the perverting influence of their self established creed, which has given birth to all the demoralizing, degrading and hellish isms, including (the last though not the least) equalityism or negrophilism.

Pardon me condeming the Yankees as a nation,
For they are not deserving eternal salvation.

H. W. R. JACKSON.

THE WOMEN

OF THE

SECOND

AMERICAN REVOLUTION.

A FEMALE SOLDIER.

Among the strange, heroic and self-sacrificing acts of woman in this struggle for our independence, we have heard of none which exceeds the bravery displayed and hardships endured by the subject of this notice, Mrs. Amy Clarke. Mrs. Clarke volunteered with her husband as a private, fought through the battles of Shiloh, where Mr. Clarke was killed—she performing the rites of burial with her own hands. She then continued with Bragg's army in Kentucky, fighting in the ranks as a common soldier, until she was twice wounded—once in the ankle and then in the breast, when she fell a prisoner into the hands of the Yankees. Her sex was discovered by the Federals, and she was regularly paroled as a prisoner of war, but they did not permit her to return until she had donned female apparel.—Mrs. C. was in our city on Sunday last, en route for Bragg's command.—*Jackson Mississippian, Dec. 30, 1862.*

A FEMALE AID-DE-CAMP.

The Baltimore "Clipper" says Antonia J. Ford was the principal spy and guide for Captain Mosbly in his recent raid on Fairfax Court House, and aided in planning the arrest of Gen. Slaughter, Wyndham and others.' She was arrested and brought to the Old Capitol Prison, on Sunday last, with $1,000 Confederate money on her person. The following is a copy of her commission:

To all whom it may Concern:

Know ye that, reposing special confidence in the patriotism fidelity and ability of Antonia J. Ford, I, J. E. B. Stuart, by virtue of power vested in me as Brigadier General, Provisional Army Confederate States, hereby appoint and commission her my Honorable Aid-de-Camp, to rank as such from this date. She will be obeyed, respected and *admired* by all lovers of a noble nature.

Given under my hand and seal, Headquarters Cavalry Brigade, at Camp Beverly, 7th October, 1861, and first year of our Independence.
J. E. B. STUART.

By the General:
L. T. BRYAN, A. A. G.

MISS BELLE BOYD, "THE REBEL SPY."

This young lady has, by her devotion to the Southern cause, called down upon her head the anathemas of the entire Yankee press.

Miss Belle is the daughter of Benjamin B. Boyd, of Martinsburg, at which place he was for a long time prominently engaged in the mercantile profession. He afterwards removed to Knoxville, Tennessee, where he lived about three years, but returned to Martinsburg about two years previous to the breaking out of the present war. Her mother was the daughter of Captain Glenn, of Jefferson county. Miss Belle is the oldest child of her parents, and is about 23 years of age. An uncle of Miss Belle, James W. Glenn, of Jefferson county, commanded a company during the present war, known as the "Virginia Rangers," until recently, the captaincy of which he resigned on account of ill-health. James E. Stuart, a prominent politician of the Valley, and who was a member of the Virginia Convention of 1850, married a sister of Miss Belle's mother.

During her early years Miss Belle was distinguished for her sprightliness and the vivacity of her temper.

That our readers may have an opportunity of seeing what the Yankee correspondents say about this young lady, we extract the following article from the columns of the Philadelphia "Inquirer," which was written by the army correspondent of that sheet:

"These women are the most accomplished in Southern circles. They are introduced under assumed names to our officers, so as to avoid detection or recognition from those to whom their names are known, but their persons unknown. By such means they are enabled to frequently meet combinedly, but at separate times, the officers of every regiment in a whole column, and by simple compilation and comparison of notes, they achieve a full knowledge of the strength of our entire force. Has modern warfare a parallel to the use of such accomplishments for such a purpose? The chief of these spies is the celebrated Belle Boyd. Her acknowledged superiority for machination and intrigue has given her the leadership and control of the female spies in the valley of Virginia. She is a resident of Martinsburg, when at home, and has a pious, good old mother, who regrets as much as any one can the violent and eccentric course of her daughter since this rebellion has broken out. Belle has passed the freshness of youth. She is a sharp-featured, black-eyed woman of 25, or care and intrigue have given her that appearance. Last summer, whilst Patterson's army lay at Martinsburg, she wore a revolver in her belt, and was courted and flattered by every Lieutenant and Captain in the service who ever saw her. There was a kind of Di Vernon dash about her, a smart pertness, a quickness of retort and utter abandonment of manner and bearing which were attractive from their very romantic unwontedness.

"The father of this resolute black-eyed vixen is a paymaster in the Southern army, and formerly held a place at Washington under our Government. She has undergone all that society, position and education can confer upon a mind suited to the days of Charles the Second, or Louis the Fourteenth—a mind such as Mazarin or Richelieu would have delighted to employ from its kindred affinities.

" Well, this woman I saw practicing her arts upon our young Lieutenants and inexperienced Captains, and in each case I uniformly felt it my duty to call them aside and warn them of whom she was. To one she had been introduced as Miss Anderson, to another as Miss Faulkner, and so to the end of the chapter. She is so well known now that she can only practice her blandishments upon new raw levies and their officers. But from them she obtains the number of their regiments and their force. She has, however, a trained band of coadjutors, who report to her daily—girls aged from 16 upward—women who have the common sense not to make themselves as conspicuous as she, and who remain unknown, save to her, and are, therefore, effective. The reports that she is personally impure are as unjust as they are undeserved. She has a blind devotion to an idea, and passes far the boundary of her sex's modesty to promote its success.

"During the past campaign in the Valley this woman has been of immense service to the enemy. She will be now if she can."—*Illustrated News.*

MISS NORAH McCARTEY.
A REMINISCENCE OF THE MISSOURI CAMPAIGN.

Thus far, Missouri has the better of other seats of hostility for the real romance of war. Most assuredly the fight there has been waged with fiercer earnest than almost anywhere else. The remote geography of the country, the rough, unhewn character of the people, the intensity and ferocity of the passions excited, and the general nature of the complicity reduced to a warfare essentially parizan and frontier, gave to its progress a wild aspect, peculiarly susceptible to deeds, and suggestive of thoughts, of romantic interest. None of these struck us more forcibly than the story of Norah McCartey, the Jennie Deans of the West.

She lived in the interior of Missouri—a little, pretty, black-eyed girl, with a soul as huge as a mountain, and a form as frail as a fairy's, and the courage and pluck of a buccaneer into the bargain. Her father was an old man—a secessionist. She had but a single brother, just growing from boyhood to youthhood, but sickly and lamed. The family had lived in Kansas during the trouble of '57, when Norah was a mere girl of fourteen, or thereabouts. But even then her beauty, wit and devil-may-care spirit were known far and wide; and many were the stories told along the border of her sayings and doings. Among other charges laid to her door, it is said she broke all the hearts of the young bloods far and wide, and tradition does even go so far as to assert that, like Bob Acres, she killed a man once a week, keeping a private church-yard for the purpose of decently burying her dead. Be this as it may, she was then, and is now, a dashing, fine looking, lively girl, and a prettier heroine than will be found in a novel, as will be seen if the good natured reader has a mind to follow us down to the bottom of this column.

Not long after the Federals came into her neighborhood, and, after they had forced her father to take the oath, which he did partly because he was a very old man, unable to take the field, and hoped thereby to save the security of his household, and partly because he could not help himself; not long after these two important events in the history of our heroine, a body of men marched up one evening, whilst she was on a visit to a neighbor's and arrested her sickly, weak brother, bearing him off to Leavenworth City, where he was lodged in the military guard-house.

It was nearly night before Norah reached home. When she did so, and discovered the outrage which had been perpetrated and the grief of her old father, her rage knew no bounds. Although the mists were falling and the night was closing in, dark and dreary, she ordered her horse to be re-saddled, put on a thick *surtout*, belted a sash round her waist, and sticking a pair of ivory-handled pistols in her bosom, started off after the soldiers. The post was many miles distant. But that she did not regard. Over hill, through marsh, under cover of the darkness, she galloped on to the headquarters of the enemy. At last the call of a sentry brought her to a stand, with a hoarse—

"Who goes there?"

"No matter," she replied, "I wish to see Col. Prince. your commanding officer, and instantly, too."

Somewhat awed by the presence of a young female on horseback at that late hour, and perhaps struck by her imperious tone of command, the Yankee guard, without hesitation, conducted her into the fortifications, and thence to the quarters of the Colonel commanding, with whom she was left alone.

"Well, madam," quoth the Yankee officer, with bland politeness, "to what have I the honor of this visit?"

"Is this Col. Prince?" replied the brave girl, quietly.

"It is, and yourself?"

"No matter. I have come here to inquire where you have a lad by the name of McCartey a prisoner?"

"There is such a prisoner."

"May I ask, for why?"

"Certainly; for being suspected of treasonable connection with the enemy."

"*Treasonable* connection with the enemy! Why, the boy is sick and lame. He is besides my brother; and I have come to ask his immediate release."

The Yankee officer opened his eyes; was sorry he could not comply with the request of so winning a supplicant; and must really beg her to desist and leave the fortress."

"I *demand* his release," cried she, in reply.

"That you cannot have," returned he; "the boy is a rebel and a traitor, and unless you retire, madam, I shall be forced to arrest you on a similar suspicion."

"Suspicion! I *am* a rebel and a traitor too, if you wish.— Young McCartey is my brother, and I don't leave this tent until he goes with me. Order his instant release, or," here she drew one of the aforesaid ivory handles out of her bosom and levelled the muzzle of it directly at him, "I will put an ounce of lead in your brain, before you can call a single sentry to your relief."

A picture that?

There stood the heroic girl; eyes flashing fire, cheek glowing with earnest will, lips firmly set with resolution, and hand outstretched with a loaded pistol ready to send the contents through the now thoroughly frightened, startled, aghast soldier, who cowered, like blank paper before flames, under her burning stare.

"Quick!" she repeated, "order his release, or you die."

It was too much. Prince could not stand it. He bade her lower her infernal weapon for God's sake, and the boy should be forthwith liberated.

"Give the order first," she replied, unmoved.

And the order was given; the lad was brought out; and drawing his arm in hers, the gallant sister marched out of the place, with one hand grasping one of his, and the other hold of her trusty ivory-handle. She mounted her horse, bade him get up behind, and rode off, reaching home without accident before midnight.

Now that is a fact stranger than fiction, which shows what

sort of metal is in our women of the much abused and traduced nineteenth century.—*Exchange.*

A BRAVE GIRL.

The Columbus (Ga.) "Times" says the following extract from a letter of a Savannah girl (not all unknown to fame) is too good to be immersed in the private portfolio for which it was intended:

Do you believe that instead of feeling frightened I feel quite brave, and I think if I only had the strength of my heart in my hand, I would make a little here during this war? On the day that the engagement was going on at Port Royal, and everything around us was one wild scene of confusion, for fear of an attack on Savannah, I seated myself in the midst of all, and made a Confederate flag for the express purpose of waving it saucily in their faces when they landed. If they come upon us by land, they will have to pass this very door, and in spite of everything but *chains* I intend to wave my banner. I intend to be the first Savannah girl to dare them, and to show them the South has not only brave *men*, but brave *women* also. How it makes my blood boil when I hear of a cowardly act done by any one bearing the name of *man!* There were *some* in Savannah who, during the fight at Port Royal, became alarmed for fear their courage might be put to the test, and as they would much rather run than fight, and could not do so well if they wore a hat and boots, preferred the more modest attire of females, and took to bonnets and slippers. Since then I have considered our uniform disgraced forever, if we do not prove to the world that *all* who wear this modest disguise are not cowards. To set the rest of the gentler sex an example, I have volunteered to exchange my hat and slippers for the boots and breeches of the next man who had rather run than fight, and promise, too, that I never will disgrace it by cowardly conduct. If the men prove cowards at a time like this, it is high time for the women to show what they can do; and if they cannot depend on them for protection, show them that they have bravery enough to meet them at their own doors, if they cannot follow them to the battle-field.

I think that every woman should prove a true Spartan to the cause of liberty, and when history shall bear record of the deeds of 1861, it will reflect upon them no disgrace, but give them credit for following the example of their mothers of '76.

FIENDISH OUTRAGE UPON WOMEN.

A deed committed by Federal soldiers has come to the knowledge of the writer, which is shocking beyond description, and the bare mention of which will produce a thrill of horror in every Southern breast. The information comes in such a shape as to leave no doubt in regard to the truth of the story.

A few years ago a young lady of Columbia, Tennessee, was married to a young lawyer of Helena, Arkansas. She was educated, talented, witty and accomplished in a high degree. We speak from personal knowledge in making this affirmation. They were comfortably settled in Helena, and was blessed with one or more children. Her husband is in the Southern army. Five Federal soldiers, including an officer, forcibly seized this lady, carried her to a barn, and each of them committed an outrage on her person. In two or three weeks she died, a victim of their brutality, and of the grief and mortification produced by their treatment of her.

Her husband is said to be a Lieutenant Colonel of some regiment. The writer knows him, and could give his name, but forbear to do so.

Soldiers and men of the South, think of this unparalleled deed of crime and infamy, and let it nerve you to fight for the protection of your wives and children, and to drive back and destroy the invaders of your country and despoilers of your homes.—*Knoxville Register*, Oct. 22, 1862.

UNPARELLELED ATROCITY OF YANKEE DEMONS.

The Shelbyville (Tenn.) "Banner" says that very recently a foraging party of the enemy, escorted by a command of cavalry, visited the premises of Mr. Anthony, in Williamson county.— The Colonel, Major and other officers entered the house and indulged in the usual freedom and license. At the same time they permitted a number of negro teamsters to seize the daughters of Mr. Anthony, and ravish these unprotected females. Their mother besought the protection of the officers, but these brutal men only cursed her, as a d—d rebel, saying that they understood that the husbands of her daughters were in the Confederate service, and they were being served properly thus to be outraged by a race they had enslaved.—*March*, 1863.

Oh! God we implore Thee to hear our prayer and aid us. Let us accord to the Yankees everlasting reproach: *aye, undying shame*. Bless us, oh Lord, to remember them with ever increasing hatred and contempt. Guide us and direct with the most deadly purpose, for their destruction, all our material and appliances of war. Enable us to avenge the many outrages they committed upon our women. Hear, oh God, my prayer, I beseech thee, and bless our armies, in every conflict, with a two-fold victory over our demented foe. Let the carnage, the destruction of life and limb in the ranks of our enemies be an hundred fold greater than heretofore known. Would that I could wield a sword of infinite magnitude, its blade keenly wetted for the vengeance of Heaven, and my arm clothed with the power of Omnipotence. H. W. R. J.

THE WOMEN OF WINCHESTER, VIRGINIA.

The New York "New World's" correspondent from Banks' retreating army, writing from Hagerstown, Maryland, says that while the Federalists were retreating through Winchester, *women* of that town opened fire with pistols upon them from the windows, "and killed a great many." It is very doubtful whether or no this is true. The women of the town hardly fired the guns. Probably they were too glad to see the Yankees going to delay the departure of even one of them by a wound from a pistol shot. The statement may, however, be taken as an indication of what the writer thinks of the women of Winchester. Their fidelity to their country was so marked that the Yankee not only expected no sympathy from them in the reverse which hurried him from Winchester, but he even feared they would give him a parting shot as he fled. So the well aimed bullets, which are alleged to have killed many of his comrades, are charged upon the ladies! But how can the Yankees hope for a restoration of the Union with a people whose women even take up arms against them? Go where they may they find the ladies firm in their devotion to the South, giving the invader no encouragement, and showing him no respect, until they have brought down upon themselves a full share of that Puritan hate which for so many months has poured out the vials of its wrath upon our country. Butler has led on the attack upon them, and cunningly devised the means by which the most depraved and brutal animosity is to be appeased. But the women of the South, like the women of Winchester, will continue true in the face of all the terrors the invader can invent. If the rougher sex were as universally faithful as the women, this great struggle would have nothing to fear from enemies at home. God save the noble ladies of the South!— None of their sex, in any age or country, ever merited in a higher degree the admiration of chivalrous men or their most glorious deeds in arms in their defence.

A SPIRITED LADY OF NORTH CAROLINA.

Under the head of "an impudent note from a Southern lady," the New Orleans "Delta" publishes the following, showing how a true Southern lady dared to beard Picayune Butler in his stronghold:

EDITORS DELTA—*Sir:* Having been arrested a few days since

for the display of Confederate colors upon my person, in commemoration of our victory in Virginia, and since released upon *unconditional* terms, I now desire through your columns to contradict the rumor of an apology having been made by me to Butler for the so-called offence.

I take the liberty of adding that I never had an interview with the above person, nor to escape punishment had to lower the dignity of our Southern principles, which I then and still represent. I am, sir, MRS. E. A. COWEN,
1862. 189 Canal street.

MURDERING WOMEN.

We learn from the exchanged prisoners who arrived here on Friday, from New Orleans, that on their departure from that city, large numbers of true-hearted Southern ladies gathered about them, waving their handkerchiefs and cheering for Jeff. Davis and the Southern Confederacy. For this the whole military force was called out and ordered to charge upon the crowd, by which four ladies were known to have been killed.

Vicksburg Citizen.

THE BAYONET! THE NEEDLE! THE PLOW!

The press, the pulpit and the purse is said to be a powerful trio, but we doubt if a stronger trio can be formed than is suggested by the caption of this article. The bayonet, the representative of our army in the field, is all important in the great work of defending our altars and hearthstones, but the army must be sustained. But for the needle, the representative of our glorious, self-sacrificing and patriotic women, how many bayonets would have been useless? How could the soldier have stood the piercing blasts and numbing frosts, without the kind ministrations of women? Her fame will be co-equal and co-extensive with that of the South—yea, will outlive it. While the bayonet has plenty of food before it in the shape of a barbarous and malignant foe, without ailment for the sturdy arm who wields it, the glistening steel is useless. It requires muscle to sustain the bayonet, and that muscle must be kept up by a fine *commissariat*. Here, then, the absolute importance of the plow, the representative of everything necessary for food, is clearly demonstrated. In vain do we send our sons and brothers to the field and supply them with clothing for the *outer* man, if the wants of the *inner* are neglected. The farmers of the Confederate States hold its independence and success in their own hands. While the weather-beaten veteran is keeping back the foe, and our women are doing their duty, let farmers not forget theirs. Let the needle and the plow then come up to the support of the bayonet.—*Atlanta Intelligencer.*

A PATRIOTIC LADY.

Lieutenant B. S. Russell, of the 16th Alabama, was of the slain at Murfreesboro', and fell in the early part of the action. When stricken down, he felt the wound to be mortal, and at once gave his sword to a comrade, saying, "take this to my wife, and tell her I died bravely." The Colonel of his regiment saw that the wish of the patriot was complied with, and, in reply to the letter, the widow, true, like all other Southern women, to the highest impulses of a noble patriotism, said: "I mourn the death of my husband, but my greatest regret is that none of his sons are old enough to take his place to battle for our liberties."

PATRIOTIC CONTRIBUTION.

A merchant of Charlotte, North Carolina, who has been in the army, and is now at home on furlough, has placed in the hands of the editor of the "Bulletin," of that place, five hundred dollars for the purchase of corn and has corn for the destitute families of soldiers in service. In a note addressed to the farmers, to which he appends the signature " X," he says:

I have had some little experience in the camps, and know by observation what is the hardest part of a soldier's life. I have seen them open their letters from home, and have witnessed the tears trickle down their cheeks as they read from home and hear of their suffering or destitute families. I tell you, if you will come forward and bring your liberal subscriptions for the support of their wives, you will make them better men and better and braver soldiers, and our country will be safer; our money better; and, above all, our consciences easier.

YANKEES OR HYENAS?

The following graphic description of our Yankees foes occurs in the late speech of President Davis on his return to Richmond from his western tour:

"Every crime conceivable, from the burning of defenceless towns to the stealing of silver forks and spoons, has marked their career. In New Orleans, Butler has exerted himself to learn the execrations of the civilized world, and now returns with his dishonors thick upon him to receive the plaudits of the only people on earth who do not blush to think he wears the human form. He has stolen millions of dollars in New Orleans from private citizens, although the usages of war exempt private property from taxation by the enemy. It is in keeping, however, with the character of the people that seeks dominion over you, claim to be your masters, to try to reduce you to subjection—give up to a brutal soldiery your towns to sack, your homes to pillage and incite servile insurrection. But in the latter point they have failed save in this that they have heaped, if possible, a deeper disgrace upon themselves. They have come to disturb your social organizations in the plea that it is a military necessity. For what are they waging war? They say to preserve the Union. Can they preserve the Union by destroying the social existence of a portion of the South? Do they hope to reconstruct the Union by striking at everything that is dear to man? By showing themselves so utterly disgraced that if the question was proposed to you whether you would combine with hyenas or Yankees, I trust every Virginian would say, give me the hyenas. [Cries of 'Good! good!' and applause."

THE VIRTUES OF WOMAN.

The fathomless wells of sensibility and sentiment which are found in the glorious history of woman, may well be said to resemble that cave located by classic historians on the summit of Mount Parnassus, on the brink of which a temple was erected and dedicated to Apollo, and into the aperture of which it is recorded that not even the goat herd could not look without being seized with fits of enthusiasm. It is woman who has cosmopolized virtue, and made it peculiar to no clime under the sun, to no race upon the face of the earth, and to no age in the calendar of time. From that dark and dismal day on which Mary passed from the foot of the cross to the door of the sepulchre, the celestial music of woman's soothing voice has been heard everywhere, all round the globe, amid the deepest gloom of sorrow, and the example of her conduct has never ceased to loom up to illustrate the true and modest grandeur of moral heroism. This will be found to be her history back to the very cradle of time; and however much patriots may lament the degeneracy of statesmanship in these days of small men, to the immortal honor of the sex it must be recorded that in her passage through the fearful ordeals which have met her footsteps everywhere in this revolution, woman has not only always sustained the exalted character which from time immemorial has been her righteous portion, but has not unfrequently rose above the brilliant examples of the past, and outshone even herself. When Francisco, Marquis of Pescari, had distinguished himself by his valor at the battle of Pavia, he was thought of importance enough to bribe, and he was offered the crown of Naples to betray his sovereign. He wrote to his wife the facts, to which she sent him the following reply: "Your virtue may raise you above the glory of being king. The sort of honor which goes down to our children with real lustre, is derived from our deeds and qualities, not from power or titles. For myself, I do not wish to be the wife of a king, but of a general, who can make himself superior to the greatest king, not only by courage, but by magnanimity and superiority to any less elevated motive than duty." Am I challenged to produce an example of virtue, born of this revolution, which is equal to this? I can do it. In 1844, a young officer from Kentucky graduated at West Point entered the United States army. His patrimony amounted to a handsome fortune, and he soon thereafter was joined in the holy bands of wedlock to a beautiful and accomplished heiress at the North, whose dowry approximated closely to a half million of dollars. When this revolution burst upon the two countries, he saw in a twinkling that if he drew his sword under the Confederate flag his own splendid patrimony, and the still more splendid fortune he had acquired by his marriage, was bound to be swept from him and his family. It could not but occur to him that he might fall in the war, and while his perception of the right to dispose of his own patrimony in the maintenance of principles was clear, it was not so easy a matter to prepare to take with him to a soldier's grave the consciousness that he had beggard a widowed wife and her orphan children, when it was to her he was indebted for so much of his estate. In this dilemma she read his thoughts, and the language—as reported to me by a lady, than whom no country contains a superior, either morally or intellectually, who heard it—in which she relieved him from his delicate embarrassment, furnishes a parallel for the reply of the wife of Francisco, and settles the fact, that in this Confederacy we have wives which are an honor to the human race. Here it is: "You say that your conscience tells you that the South is right. Let not the sacrifice then of any portion, or all of the fortune you acquired by our marriage prevent you from sustaining the true dignity of your character, either in your estimation or in the eyes of our God. Our fortune is ample, but there is no fortune in the world equal in value to a conscientious husband. Moreover, I, too, believe the South is right, and therefore, albeit the North get our estate, let the South have your sword. The pleasure that we will derive from doing right, and the fame that you will acquire by the sacrifices that you will make and the services you will render to the Confederate cause, will be worth more to us while we live, and to our children hereafter, than any paltry fortune we could possess or they could from us inherit, when we are gone.

That husband instantly espoused our cause. At the fall of Fort Donelson he was among the prisoners who fell into the hands of the enemy. His heroic and noble wife applied to Gen. Sherman, at Cairo, to ascertain the whereabouts of her husband and for permission to visit him. The requests were respectively met with a categorical and brutal refusal, but she was informed, while no information could be given her of where her husband was, still if she desired to visit her friends at the North she would be permitted to do so. "Sir," said she, "the only friend

I have at the North whom I ever wish to see again is my husband, Gen. B., and if I cannot be permitted to see him I have no further request to make."

Who can compute the value of such incidents in the instruction they furnish to the world, of who we as a people are, and how is that instruction to be imparted if from a false sense of delicacy we refuse to allow the light of such incidents to shine!

Advertiser & Register.

WHAT CAN WOMAN DO?

BY A. V. S.

I see the satirical smile resting upon your features, Sir Cynic, as you slowly unfold the paper and see the commencement of this sketch. Don't think I am about to commence a labored discussion upon *woman's rights*, and thereby bore you to death with philosophical nonsense. Nothing of the kind, I assure you, is my intention; for woman, in the stern character of lecturer upon the rostrum and stage, we will leave to be personated by the strong-minded woman of the North, and turn our eyes to a more extended field of labor in our own *Sunny South.*

Neither do I wish to present her in the light of a ball-room belle—a mere parlor ornament—whose highest ambition is to expend large sums annually in decorating her person and feeding her insatiate vanity; playing occasionally a little miserable music; smattering a good deal of odious French, and flirting desperately with every moustached foreigner who chances to fall into her clutches.

From both of these pictures we turn, in absolute disgust, to woman's true, only proper sphere, as the brightener of man's existence; the one star, whose radiance far transcends all other earthly objects. The influence a pure-hearted woman exerts over the world at large, can never be adequately known. Little deeds of kindness, soft words of friendship whispered into the ear of some lonely, forlorn one, may be the means of raising his spirits from the depths of despondency, giving an impetus to his nobler, higher powers, and causing him to go forth into the great battle of life with renewed energy.

What more beautiful than to see her, unlike the gay devotee of fashion, turning her attention from the allurements of pleasure to that *home* which she can so well beautify and adorn. It is her world, in which she is monarch of all she surveys. What an exalted and dignified position? The idol of every heart, she rules by the kindness and love which, like incense, rises all around her happy pathway. When the bright beams of prosperity's sun are obscured, and poverty's dark cloud enshrouds man's horizon, then it is that woman's love appears as a beacon light, shedding its brilliant rays far o'er life's dreary water, brightening every object, until nothing seems too difficult for the renewed spirit; labor rather a pleasure.

Every other friend may forsake, and turn away, in the sad hour of affliction; but 'tis then with woman that her nature, like the ivy around the sturdy oak, entwines more closely, and strives more faithfully to bind up the bleeding tendrils of the weary heart of father, brother or husband. No hand like her's can lift, as with magic, the shade of care from a loved one's brow, can speak those sweet words of comfort so grateful to the bowed spirit, can lead, by cheerful conversation, the thoughts away from disagreeable subjects, and make him forget that aught save truth, purity and love ever mingles with our lot on earth.

She could be dispensed with everywhere better than in a *sick-room*. There is woman's particular forte more plainly visible than anywhere else. The lords of creation may boast extravagantly of their independence, but when the heavy hand of disease is laid upon their frames, and the strong man becomes as a little child in weakness, then he must acknowledge his reliance upon *her care*. Who is there besides that can so well bathe the fevered brow, raise the cooling draught to the parched lips, and bestow all of those little nameless attentions which would only be thought of by a woman? Night after night will she sit, a lone watcher, by the couch of pain, bearing the fretful exclamations of man's turbulent nature with patience, striving, as best she can, to mitigate his sufferings and allowing herself, sometimes, no rest, for her wearied system. Self is entirely forgotten for the time, and the one great thought of doing good for the loved suffering one seems to absorb her every faculty.

Well indeed has the poet said:

> "O, woman! in our hours of ease,
> Fantastic, coy and hard to please,
> And variable as the shade
> By the light quivering aspen made:
> When pain and anguish wring the brow,
> A ministering angel thou."

How sublime is woman in the character of mother. 'Tis her's to lead the infant minds of those committed to her care to noble thoughts of existence; and upon the unwritten tablets of their young hearts, inscribed, with indelible distinctness, those lessons which, in after years, never can be forgotten. The father of his country, our own beloved Washington, owed his success, in life, to that mother whose precepts he treasured within his heart, and which he never failed to respect even when he was at the pinacle of glory and idolized by a grateful people. Throughout all ages so powerful has been the influence of a mother upon the lives of their sons, that in reading the histories of great men, one never fails to be struck with this peculiar power. It is the talisman which causes them, when everything else fails to move, to repent of their transgressions and abandon the paths of vice forever. Even though years may have passed since that loved voice was hushed in death, yet never will conscience fail to upbraid when her teachings are about to be disobeyed. When the path of glory invites, at her warning voice that slippery course is abandoned, and the conqueror is again a *child*. Coriolanus, enraged at the treatment he had received at the hands of his countrymen, after joining his enemies, marched upon the city of Rome. All would have been lost—the beautiful seven-hilled city would have been razed to the ground—but his *mother*, with a band of maidens, went out to him and entreated his forbearance. The strong man burst into tears, and exclaimed: "*Mother, you have saved Rome, but lost your son!*"—*Illustrated News*, February, 1863.

"GOD'S LAST, BEST GIFT TO MAN," WOMAN A MINISTERING ANGEL.

It is always cheering and encouraging to the patriot soldier to receive the approving smiles of lovely woman, how much so, when to these are added delicate attentions, profuse hospitality and angelic liberality. Such was the good fortune of the *Marion Rifles*, when ordered to Rocky Point, North Carolina. The attentions then and there received from "God's last, best gift to man," are indelibly engraved upon the tablets of our memories and hearts, and will always be most fondly cherished. The warm and friendly greeting, the pressing, ready welcome, the delightful hours, spent in social intercourse, all combined to render our sojourn there, not only pleasant and happy, but satisfied us that indeed we were among "ministering angels."

New Year's day, 1863, at Rocky Point, will always be gratefully commemorated by us as a corps, and fond memory will oftimes bring to mind the actors of that day. The Rev. Mr. H., the widow M., the fascinating Mrs. H. and her lovely sister, Mrs. C., as also the dear little spirits, Misses Sallie H. and Lizzie C., and we cannot omit our bachelor friend, Mr. B.—all were intent upon making us happy and at home; what associations cluster in that word, sweet, sweet home. We wish these kind friends continued happiness and prosperity, and indulge the sincere hope that their quiet and happy homes may be undisturbed by the desecrating Abolitionists, but should he threaten them, we would accept with proud and happy distinction the privilege of being the foremost to meet and drive off, at any sacrifice, the enemy of our country and happiness.

MARION RIFLES.

BEAUTIFUL EULOGIUM AND TRIBUTE TO WOMAN— WOMAN'S HEROISM.

* * * The attitude of woman is sublime. Bearing all the sacrifices of which I have just spoken, she is moreover called upon to suffer in her affections, to be wounded and smitten where she feels deepest and most enduringly. Man goes to the battle-field, but woman sends him there, even though her heartstrings tremble while she gives the farewell kiss and the farewell blessing. Man is supported by the necessity of movement, by the excitement of action, by the hope of honor, by the glory of conquest. Woman remains at home to suffer, to bear the cruel torture of suspense, to tremble when the battle has been fought, and the news of the slaughter is flashing over the electric wire, to know that defeat will cover her with dishonor and her little ones with ruin, to learn that the husband she doated upon, the son whom she cherished in her bosom, and upon whom she never let the wind blow too rudely, the brother with whom she sported through all her happy days of childhood, the lover to whom her early vows were plighted, has died upon some distant battle-field, and lies there a mangled corpse, unknown and uncared for, never to be seen again, even in death! Oh! those fearful lists of the wounded and the dead! How carelessly we pass them over, unless our own loved ones happen to be linked with them in military association, and yet each name in that roll of slaughter carries a fatal pang to some woman's heart—some noble devoted woman's heart. But she bears it all, and bows submissively to the stroke. He died for the cause. He perished for his country. I would not have it otherwise, but I should like to have given the dying boy my blessing, the expiring husband my last kiss of affection, the bleeding lover the comfort of knowing that I kneeled beside him. * * * * *

Extract from a sermon delivered in Christ's Church, Savannah, Georgia, December, 1862.

THE SOCIETY OF WOMAN.

No society is more profitable, because none more refining and provocative of virtue, than that of refined and sensible women. God enshrined peculiar goodness in the form of women, that her beauty might win, her gentle voice invite, and the desire of her favor persuade men's sterner souls to leave the paths of sinful strife for the ways of pleasantness and peace. But when woman falls from her blest eminence, and sinks the guardian and the cherisher of pure and rational enjoyments into the vain coquette, and flattered idolator of idle fashion, she is unworthy of an honorable man's love, or a sensible man's admiration.— Beauty is then but, at best,

"—— A pretty play thing,
Dear deceit."

We honor the chivalrous deference which is paid in our land to woman. It proves that our men know how to respect virtue and pure affection, and that our women are worthy of such respect. Yet woman should be something more than mere woman to win us to their society. To be our companions, they should be fitted to be our friends; to rule our hearts, they should be deserving the approbation of our minds. There are many such, and that there are not more, is rather the fault of our sex than their own; and despite all the unmanly scandals that have been thrown upon them in prose or verse, they would rather share in the rational conversation of men of sense than listen to the silly compliments of fools; and a man dishonors them, as well as disgraces himself, when he seeks their circle for idle pastime, and not for the improvement of his mind and the elevation of his heart.

TO ALL SOUTHERN LADIES.

Earnest devotion of the ladies of the South. Did but our men manifest the same ardor our final success would not be withheld much longer.

The following resolutions were adopted at a female prayer meeting at Carrolton, Alabama, and their publication was requested:

WHEREAS, Almighty God, in his infinite wisdom, has permitted a cruel, unholy and destructive war to come upon us as a scourge for our sinfulness and wanderings from Him; and believing that the Omnipotent Arm alone can save us from the impending dangers; therefore, the ladies of Carrolton, at their female prayer meeting, resolved that they would set apart a half hour the first Monday in every month, for *special prayer for peace*, and ask every lady throughout the South to engage with us. We do not make this request because we think Christians are not praying; for we believe there has never been a time when more earnest prayers were offered up for the same purpose, and never has there been so great a necessity for *importunate* prayer as now. We believe our people are becoming humbled, and it is the best indication of peace we have had, but we are not humble enough yet. God is a prayer-hearing and a prayer-answering God. Then let every woman's heart be united in prayer. Let each wife, mother and sister retire at sunset (on the above mentioned day,) and beseech the Lord to save us from our cruel enemies, to watch over, preserve and restore to us our beloved ones; and grant us a speedy and honorable peace. We consider prayer the most powerful of *all* weapons.

The very idea of so many being engaged in prayer the same hour is impressive of itself; we think it would encourage many a poor soldier to look forward with pleasing hopes for peace and a safe return to his beloved ones.

All papers favorable to this proposition will please copy.

A LADY.

The ladies, God bless them, are the true patriots in this struggle; for while the *pseudo* lords of creation are gambling in the prime necessaries of life, causing fear and trembling to seize even the most sanguine well-wisher of the Southern cause, the fair sex, as ministering angels, are pouring oil on the troubled waters, and doing their utmost in assistance to bring about an honorable peace, by rendering the soldier comfortable, and thereby nerving his arm, so that he may be able to withstand the rigors of the winter and successfully contend against fearful odds on the battle-field.

WHY NOT IMPORT PROVISIONS?

Mr. Editor: I often see and hear the remark made, that "we have but one thing to fear in our present struggle, but one thing that will conquer, ruin us, which is the failure of the grain crop." All acknowledge that to be an event of such moment, that its occurrence would most inevitably ruin us. Still, I see no effort making to meet such a startlingly frightful calamity; but 'tis left to time to develope the awful uncertainty of our salvation or our destruction. I may be asked what plan have I to offer that will give us a certainty over the future. I cannot say I have any such suggestion to make. But one thing appears strange to me. In looking over the catalogues of the cargoes of those vessels which succeed in eluding the blockaders, they are assorted, to be sure, but in vain does the patriot search for the staff of life—breadstuffs. We find silk, merino, broad cloth, hoop skirts, alpaca, tea, &c., &c., &c., each and every one of which articles we can do without. Our independence can be achieved, I may say, better without than with them, as well as numerous other articles which fill the aforesaid catalogues.

Can no inducement be offered to men engaged in this business tempting enough to cause them to invest their money in the great necessaries of life? I would say, let a premium be offered by our Government for every barrel of flour and every pound of bacon, and, if found advisable and practicable, levy a heavy revenue upon the unnecessaries, which are now purchased by the fashionable and luxury lovers of our land at enormous prices. Aye, yes, let the inducement be such that no vessel would b freighted for our shores with aught but bread, meat, medicine and army stores. Flood our land, if possible, with the aforesaid articles, but, above all, bread, and we are saved. Yes, I say above all bread, for it is even more necessary to our success than ammunition. I may be told but a small quantity can reach us in this way. Well, even if small, it would be that much help; but I feel confident that much would reach us. Take, for instance, the amount which one firm alone, that of Fraser & Co., of Charleston, has realized from this business—ten millions, (eight millions of which have been invested in Confederate bonds—all honor to them), and then tell me the quantity would be small. Not to speak of what others have made by similar investments, which, if taken into account, would swell these figures to an almost fabulous amount, an amount which, even at the high price of flour and meat now, would purchase a sufficiency to warrant an escape from famine, should our crops fail— a contingency so awful, that I tremble as I contemplate it. I almost idolize my country, and this is the only apology I have to offer for obtruding this suggestion upon the public.

A DAUGHTER OF THE SOUTH.

ATROCITIES OF THE FEDERALS.

A correspondent of the Chicago "Times" writing from Memphis, gives the following account of the cold blooded and unprovoked murder of a Mr. C. W. Alexander:

But, to satisfy you that I am not fabricating, imposing upon your readers, let me narrate, in a few words, three occurrences which have taken place within the last week in this city. A host of witnesses stand ready to corroborate what I shall say. The first case was that of a gentleman by the name of C. W. Alexander. He was going to his residence in the suburbs of the city, when a cavalry soldier rode up to him. The first word uttered came from the soldier. "You are a deserter," he said. "You are mistaken," replied Mr. A., "I am a citizen of this place, and if you will but step with me to the top of the hill, I will satisfy you by the pickets there, who know me well, that I live here, for they see me every day." "Well, you are a damned Secessionist, then," said the soldier. "That is a question I do not propose to discuss here," was the reply; and Mr. Alexander, being ordered to go ahead, started. He had gone but a few steps, when the soldier drew a pistol and shot him in the back, the ball passing entirely through the body. He sank down immediately, was soon taken up by friends and carried home, where he lingered about three days before he died.

Scarcely two weeks elapse ere the brother of the deceased is assassinated by one of Lincoln's fiendish hirelings. The Jackson "Appeal," of the 17th, has the following:

The Memphis "Argus" has information that Mr. J. M. Alexander, formerly of the firm of Foster & Alexander, was killed at Fulton, Tennessee, a few days ago, by a soldier. No particulars of the affair have reached Memphis. Mr. Alexander was a brother of Mr. C. W. Alexander, who was shot in the northern portion of the city a few weeks ago.

The correspondent of the Chicago "Times," after narrating the first murder, continues:

Somewhere about the same time, some soldiers noticed a boy, who was not observing them. One of them, drawing his revolver, remarked that he believed he could hit the boy, and, suiting the action to the word, fired, shooting him through the hip. It is thought the wound will terminate mortally.

YANKEE BRUTALITY.

The Richmond "Dispatch" gives the following account of Yankee brutality in Norfolk:

We have been shown a private letter from a lady, in Norfolk, giving an account of the arrest and search of three ladies of that city by the Federal authorities. The writer of the letter being one of the victims to this piece of Yankee malignity, rehearses her treatment with an indignation characteristic of insulted womanly virtue. The Provost Marshal, it seems, shirked the responsibility of the contemptible proceeding, and left the matter in the hands of a set of unprincipled clerks, who secured the services of a woman as bankrupt in morals as themselves to superintend the search. Against only one of these ladies was there any charge, and she was arrested upon information furnished to the 19th Wisconsin regiment by a negro that she intended to pass the lines with letters for parties in the Confederate army. When she was taken before the Provost Marshal the other two ladies went to see her, when all three were subjected to a rigid examination in a room adjoining the Marshal's office.

AN APPEAL FROM WOMEN.

A call has been made upon all the able-bodied men to come at once to the rescue of our country, and some one has asked that we, the women, use our influence in urging forward to duty those who have not been prompt to respond to the call.

We have tried to do our duty in this great struggle for liberty. In every way except by personal appeals; by our labor and conduct throughout, we have exhorted, urged and encouraged our natural protectors, to shield us from subjugation by our tyrannical foes; and with loving hearts, willing hands and tearful eyes, we have labored night and day to prepare food, clothing, and everything we could to relieve our suffering soldiers, and otherwise aid our cause. Physically, we are weak and timid; and though the loved ones we have sent into the service are dear to us as our heart's blood, their honor is dearer than life itself.

All know how intensely women admire courage in men. It is impossible for us to respect a coward, and every true woman who has husband, father, brother or lover—though he be the sun of her existence—the one star of her hope, had rather see him prostrate before her with death's signet on his noble brow that has never been branded by cowardice or dishonor, than have him forfeit his good name and disgrace his manhood, by refusing to do his duty to his country. Women would have men love God first, their country next, and then herself.

We know the longer the war lasts the more homes will be desolated; the more precious lives will be lost by disease and battle; and if the war continues long, all will be compelled to go into the service and do their duty; and we prefer that all should go now—go without further delay, and with one effectual blow, and at once, this cruel war, which is desolating our country and rending our hearts. If we must be left alone and unprotected at our homes, be it so. If we suffer it will be in a good cause, and God and His Holy Angels will take care of those who trust in Him.

If left to the women of the South to decide, we say, if it be necessary, let all go at once. The sooner the war is ended, the sooner will our sufferings be over; we, therefore, implore every man, who is able to bear arms, to go forth and wield them in our defence. You are politically, as well as naturally, our protectors. We look to you; we cling to you as our earthly hope—our only dependence. You know that your lives are dear to us. Oh! so dear! But your lives cease to be dear to us, when you fail to provide us a country that we can be proud of, and when we can no longer reverence your honor, your patriotism and your courage. This patriotism, honor and courage, we look to you to preserve untarnished, and to give us a country where freedom shall dwell, virtue be respected, and which will be exalted and honored among the nations of the earth. Let us have these, or let us share with you your honored graves where the bones of heroes repose. Better death than dishonor. Better the extinction of a proud race of freemen, than have a country from which liberty has taken its flight forever! Some good angel has whispered it into our hearts that Southern men can never be conquered by any foe if they will only be true to themselves and the proud national birthright which we possess; but if they prove themselves unworthy this princely heritage of freemen, liberty will bow its regal head with shame and depart from us forever.

Then, respond to our country's call, men of the South. It is woman that **pleads** and asks you to come to her rescue. Each one of you is the star—the centre of hope—of some pure woman's heart; but where will be her joy, if she see that star set forever in infamy and disgrace, either personal or national.

It is not brave, just and honorable, for some to endure all the sufferings, hardships, toils and death, which are the last of a soldier, in securing our independence for the enjoyment of others who have avoided the post of honor and danger, and have not contributed their part in this great struggle.

Come then, from the halls of learning. Come from the pulpit, the rostrum, the tripod, the counting-house, the physicians' office, come from the fields, mountains and vales. Let the great heart of the South, like the pulsations of a convulsed world, throb to the music-chimes of freedom's pealing strains, and every brave man respond to the clarion call which summons freemen to arms. Let every strong arm strike a simultaneous blow for liberty and independence. Then, indeed, we shall be free.

No matter what the position or rank you fill. Every true woman has more respect and admiration for the poor private in rags and bleeding feet, if he be a true, unselfish patriot, than for all the tinsel and gilded greatness of a laggard or coward.

We hope all will appreciate the sacrifices which we make in giving up the objects of our love; but let all understand that woman can never counsel dishonor. We will cheerfully endure the privations and sufferings that may befall us. We will still try to do our duty; labor for, assist, relieve and encourage our brave defenders; and though our hearts are torn; though we are bereft of our dearest ones, we will never say "hold! it is enough!" till the last vile foe shall bite the dust, or is driven from our soil, and our country proudly takes her place among the nations of the earth. WOMEN OF THE SOUTH.

BITTER FEMALE SECESSIONISTS.

We get the following good anecdote from the Washington correspondence of a New York paper:

Four young gentlemen, who have been residing in Alexandria for some months, a few days ago engaged apartments of a highly respectable lady in Prince street, with her two daughters, aged respectively sixteen and eighteen.

Although the lady and her daughters were open and avowed Secessionists, the former having two sons in the Confederate army, the young gentlemen were, nevertheless, surprised to hear them speaking so contemptuously and bitter of the Union.

The young gentlemen, it appears, took it into their heads to hoist the stars and stripes on the top of their dwelling one day, upon which the lady and her daughters, when they discovered it peacefully floating above them raised a storm of indignation.

One of the young ladies then clambered to the roof of the house at the risk of life or limb, and with the spirit of tigress, tore down our national flag, trampled it beneath her feet, and then threw the fragments into the stove. Not content with this disrespect, this young traitoress took the ashes of the burned flag and pitched them contemptuously into the street.

ARTFUL DODGE.

We have heard of a fellow in Bedford, whose pluck and patriotism not being of the first order, set his wits to work to devise some means to get himself exempted. At last he hit upon the plan of putting some two or three dozen bees in the leg of his pantaloons, and on the day before the meeting of the board he put the plan in execution. On the day of meeting he had himself conveyed to Liberty, where the board was sitting, and, upon examination by two doctors learned in physic, his legs were found terribly swollen. Inquiry was made of the sufferer as to how long he had been afflicted, and upon his answering for several years, the doctors pronounced him unfit for service, and he was accordingly exempted. His wife, however, with a loquacity for which we suppose she gets no thanks from the would be exempt, let the cat out of the bag, and the trick coming to the knowledge of the board, the fellow was again summoned, and upon his examination the swelling before pronounced incurable had disappeared. He was served as his cowardly conduct merited, and forced into the ranks whether or not.—*Lynchburg Republican.*

ACTS OF KINDNESS AND DEVOTION OF THE LADIES OF LOUISVILLE, KENTUCKY.

In Camp at Manchester, Tennessee, }
February, 7, 1863. }

A chaplain who remained with our wounded who were left at Murfreesboro', when we retired from that place, has arrived here. Before returning to our lines he went to Louisville, and describes, in touching language, a visit to Cavehille Cemetery, near that city. He was carried to that lovely city of the dead by a noble hearted citizen of Louisville, whose liberality and energy have given a proper burial to every Confederate soldier that has died in the city. Here, on the Northern border of Kentucky, he beheld a sight that should put to shame many who inhabit cities farther South. The grave of every Confederate was raised, sodded, and not a few surrounded with flowers. The name of the soldier, his State, and regiment, was lettered in black on a neat white head-board, around which hung a wreath of myrtle, the Christmas offering of the true Southern ladies of Louisville, to the noble dead. In the grounds allotted to the burial of the Federal dead, he found the graves sunken and uncared fored for; but few having stones or boards, or marks of any kind.

The Yankee Congress has passed an act punishing with fine and imprisonment, any one caught corresponding with a rebel. Another is added to the previously existing trials of the mothers, wives and sisters of the Kentuckians in our army. I sincerely hope their devotion to our cause may be repaid by an early release from Lincoln's hated rule. VOLUNTEER.

MOURN THOU LAND OF FLOWERS—BANISHMENT OF FAMILIES FROM ST. AUGUSTINE, FLORIDA—INHUMAN TREATMENT OF WOMEN AND CHILDREN—THE FEDERALS AT NEW ORLEANS.

We yesterday had an interview with the lady of an esteemed citizen of Savannah, who, with her family of five little children, has just arrived from St. Augustine. She gives an account of Yankee barbarism, and the hardships she had to encounter in her efforts to reach her home in this city.

In the early part of September, a meeting of the citizens of St. Augustine, male and female, from the age of fourteen years and upwards, was ordered by General Saxon to assemble at the Presbyterian Church. The meeting being assembled at the appointed time, Colonel Beard, of the Provost Guard, opened his address as follows: "I do not know whether to address you (ladies present,) as *ladies* or *women*, as all Broadway crinolined women are called *ladies!*" It was soon ascertained, from the speaker's remarks that the object of the meeting was to have the oath of allegiance to the United States administered. A guard was stationed at the door to prevent any from leaving. Those who refused to take the oath were required to go in the galleries—some two to three hundred men, women and children. The others were furnished with certificates and allowed to depart. Those from the galleries were then called down to receive, as Colonel Beard termed it, their "benediction." They were forced to register their names, together with the number of their respective residences. This having been gone through with, he told them that when he was ready he would give all the women and children among them who had relatives in the Confederacy, "a free ride across the lines."

He then gave orders to the guard to permit the ladies to pass to their homes. Their residences were duly labeled, and about a week after the meeting, wagons were sent for their baggage, and these banished people were taken on board a transport. The steamer left for the St. John's river with some fifty families—about one hundred and fifty women and children huddled together, without a bed to rest on, or any accommodations whatever, and kept two and a half days outside without food or water save what they took with them, and in their sickness were refused even water to drink. Fearing to enter the St. John's, as our informant supposes, they were taken back to St. Augustine, and when near that place it was ascertained that the vessel was leaking badly, having some four feet of water in the hold. It was supposed on board that the negroes had attempted to scuttle the vessel in order to drown the "Secesh."

Our informant, who was among the sufferers, having been furnished a pass which had been sometime previously promised her was placed with her young charge and her baggage in a cart and taken across the country to the St. John's river. The cart having broken down several times on the way, they were forced to walk and seek shelter in a negro cabin, with nothing but the naked floor to sleep upon, their feet and limbs sore and bruised, and their dresses torn by briars. Arriving at the St. Johns, they were taken across in a small boat, where they procured another cart and reached the railroad at Trail Ridge. They were, after severe suffering, some ten days in their trouble to get to our lines. Taking the railroad they came by way of Lake City, and reached this city, to the great joy of themselves and friends, Saturday evening last.

General Mitchell sent notice from Hilton Head to St. Augustine, previous to her leaving, that he would send a boat to that place and take all the ladies, who had refused to take the oath, to Jacksonville.

She states that the poor of St. Augustine are regularly furnished with rations by the Federals; but it was rumored they intended to stop the supply.

The troops are respectful to the ladies, in passing them in the streets, and are very orderly.

The soldiers are kept in their quarters at St. Francis Barracks, which is in the south end of the city, and in Fort Marion in the north end.

There is but one regiment in St. Augustine, the 7th New Hampshire, Colonel Putnam, comprising eight hundred men, and a cavalry corps.

Colonel Beard is in command of the Provost Guard, and Captain Durgin is the Provost Marshal.

During the day one company is stationed at the barracks, one at the Planters' Hotel, one on the Hill at Fort Marion, and the remainder of the regiment, except the pickets, in the Fort.

A gallant Captain of one of the companies in riding out a short time ago, beyond the pickets, lost his way and was fired upon by guerillas. He made good his escape after losing his sword, and his horse being shot. Arriving in the city with his revolver in his hand, he stated his misfortune, but boasted that he thought he killed three guerillas with his revolver.

The Federal officers in St. Augustine boasted that their Government intended to take Charleston, Savannah and Mobile this winter. They expressed the hope that when the demand was made for the surrender of Savannah it would be given up. As there were many Northern people and much Northern property in this city, they did not wish to shell it; but if the surrender was refused, they would be compelled to destroy the city.

No articles of gold or silver will be allowed to leave the city in the baggage of those who are sent away, which is regularly searched, in order to prevent them getting into the hands of the Confederates to be coined into money.

Groceries of all kinds are selling at very low figures, for gold and silver only. She saw no paper currency in circulation.

Savannah Republican, October 14, 1862.

A CRY FOR VENGEANCE—LATE FROM MISSOURI.

The editor of the Jackson "Crisis" has seen a gentleman direct from Missouri, whose reliability he vouches for, and learns from him the following interesting intelligence from that oppressed State:

The true-hearted Southern people of the State are as hopeful and sanguine of the final success of our cause as our brave soldiers here in the army. The people do not feel that they are part and parcel of the Lincoln empire, but are waiting patiently for the day to arrive when they can openly avow their allegiance to the Confederacy. The late elections in the State, in which the abolitionists were successful, have only caused the people to set a higher estimate upon the value of Southern independence. The sentiments of the true Southern people have not been changed by the tyranny of a military government, while the eyes of many of the former Union men have been opened to see the enormity of Federal usurpations, and their views have been accordingly changed.

The late elections, he says, do, by no means, reflect the sentiment of the people; but a few, comparatively, of the Southern men participated in the election—where they did vote, they voted for men known to be Southern in sentiment.

Deniphan and Wolf, the Senator and Representative during Gen. Price's stay in north-west Missouri, took their negroes to Arkansas and left them there, while they returned home to enjoy quiet and peace. Whilst the canvass was going on in Platte, Curtis went into Arkansas, seized their negroes and freed them.

In Clay, James H. Moss commands a Federal regiment, and is stationed at Liberty. Colonel Doniphan is pursuing his old course, taking no active part either one way or the other.

In Buchanan, Willard P. Hall is Brigadier General commanding the militia of the district. He superseded B. F. Loan, who was elected to Congress. Hall is also Lieutenant Governor of the State under the Provisional Government. Colonel Wm. R.

Pennick, in command of a regiment of militia, not long since left St. Joseph with his troops, in search of "bushwackers," and having reached Clay county, arrested Charles Pullins, who left Buchanan in company with Captain Gibson for the Southern army. Pullins was taken to Liberty, a mock trial was gone through with, and he was condemned to be hung. He offered to prove that he was a regularly enlisted Confederate soldier, but was denied the privilege and accordingly hung.

After hanging Pullins, Pennick proceeded two or three miles further, and found two men sitting in a widow's door. He asked them if they knew of the whereabouts of any "bushwackers." Upon being answered in the negative, he proceeded a short distance when he was attacked, and his regiment repulsed by men concealed in the brush. Pennick immediately returned to the widow's house, hung the two men he had seen there and burned the widow's house. Crossing the river into Jackson county, nominally in search of Quantrel, some of his men arrested a boy who was taking clothes to Quantrel's command. They went to the house of the boy's mother, who was a widow, seized and hung both her and her son. This man, Pennick, disgraces the position of the Most Worshipful Grand Master of the Masonic fraternity in Missouri.

We regret to learn that Captain Boyd, of St. Joseph, and Captain Hart, who so gallantly upheld the standard of Missouri, during the campaign of 1861-62, died of wounds received at Independence last August. They were Confederate officers. Henry M. Voorhees, Esq., of St. Joseph, was defeated as the pro-slavery candidate for the Legislature by the Abolitionists and weak-kneed Southerners.

In Clinton county the notorious James H. Birch is "covorting" as usual. James H. Birch, Jr., is in command at Plattsburg.

The prices of articles will look strange to some in the South. Crops of every description were abundant—better than for several years. Corn sells at $1.25 per barrel of five bushels, pork $2.50, bacon 6 to 8 cents, coffee 50 cents, sugar 25 cents, wheat 70 cents, hemp $3 to $3.50, tobacco high and stock of all kinds commanding a high price. Gold is very scarce, but "greenbacks" are very abundant and at a heavy discount.

All the county seats are garrisoned by militia, the Federal troops having been entirely withdrawn. This gentleman thinks it the height of folly for Missourians to think of returning home until our army is thrown into the State.

He says, also, that the families of all absent Southern soldiers are well attended to, and are not permitted to suffer for any of the comforts of life. No Missouri soldier need fear that his family is in want of anything to render them comfortable.

HOME FOR INVALID LADIES—INTERESTING CORRESPONDENCE—WOMAN ALWAYS FOREMOST IN PROMOTING A GOOD CAUSE—GOD BLESS HER EFFORTS WITH SUCCESS.

From the Atlanta Intelligencer.

TO THE CITIZENS OF ATLANTA.

ATLANTA, March 11, 1863.

Mr. Editor: In yesterday's issue of the "Commonwealth," I notice a report of various donations for the "Ladies' Home," from Mrs. J. N. Simmons, President of the Finance Committee; and, also, that Miss Fannie Holmes and myself had kindly offered our services to canvass Atlanta, I simply state that I am proud of an agency in a cause so noble, and that in a few days we shall commence the delightful task.

I have, in connection with other ladies, done all that was in my power to do for the soldier; but while in doing this, I neither can, nor will turn a deaf ear to the ways and means of affording relief to the afflicted of our own sex—whom we should especially cherish. Noble-hearted ladies! I love and trust that due sympathy is exercised towards every worthy female. Thousands of our ladies every year are dropping from the stage of action into premature graves for want of the advantages which can be realized in such an institution as Professor Powell proposes to build.

The ladies of our proud and devoted country have done the greater part for our independence. They have sent forth their sons into the field of battle—a host now fighting for our rights and institutions—what a sacrifice? I ask, where is the gentleman or lady that would withhold his or her mite to make these mothers and daughters independent of a common foe. Is there one nation disposed to offer us the hand of friendship? No, no! The necessity of our institution is then a settled point, and I hope our intelligent gentlemen and ladies will appreciate my efforts to aid in the institution we so much need, and that will reflect so much credit on the generosity of Southerners. We hope our philanthropic gentlemen will give liberally, which we shall receive as a token of their esteem—affection—indeed, love for the ladies of our Confederacy, Our institution we must have, we will have, and as Atlanta is the place to give it birth, why withhold the petty sum that shall usher into this city an institution of so much intrinsic value—one so honorable.

We know Professor Powell and the elevated position he holds in our Medical College, in which he has so eminently sustained himself. We know him in our families as a valuable practitioner of medicine. We know him as a man of christian character, and one of inestimable worth, and since his services can be procured in an institution of immense responsibility, is there one who will refuse to aid in an enterprise so elevated, so noble. I trust your inclinations will prompt you to a liberal subscription. Any person subscribing twenty dollars or more, as will be seen by Mrs. Simmons' Circular, will receive one copy of the book worth ten dollars, and credited with a donation of the amount received, minus ten dollars.

There are hundreds of ladies in the Confederacy that might offer to Mrs. J. N. Simmons their services to act as agents for the "Ladies' Home"—securing credit to themselves and benefit to an enterprise so benevolent.

Institutions of this nature have very many years since been established in the North, and have been productive of much good—consequently many of our ladies have sought relief from the various maladies with which they have been afflicted in those institutions; but the time has come that we are thrown upon our own resources. Then why not commence at once this benevolent, valuable and honorable work in our midst. Why linger. It must be done—it shall be done. Let these words be prophetic, and aid us so far as lies in your power, feeling assured that the liberal hand becomes the rich.

ABBY FOOT FARRAR.

Correspondence of the Macon Telegraph.
HOME FOR INVALID LADIES.
ATLANTA, GA., March 7, 1863.

Mr. Joseph Clisby: The Ladies of the Finance Committee have read with much pleasure your very kind and complimentary letter, written in behalf of the Editorial Convention, and in response to their own addressed to that intelligent body of gentlemen. Please present to them through your paper our grateful thanks for the cordial and flattering manner in which our communication was received, and for the resolutions so promptly taken to aid in the enterprise submitted to their consideration. We were satisfied that an appeal from the pen of woman, if it did not succeed in moving others, would never fall unheeded upon the ears of the intelligent gentlemen who preside over our high-toned Southern press, and failing to find friends in *them*, we would, indeed, think there were none "to do us reverence."

Your compliments to the worth and patriotism of Southern women are gratefully and fully appreciated, and it thrills our hearts with pride and pleasure to know that we can accept them as our "meed" from our noble countrymen, and feel that we have tried to make ourselves worthy the high appreciation of those to whom we look for help and defence. It is one of woman's highest pleasures to find that her noble and praiseworthy efforts are appreciated by gentlemen of worth and intelligence, but in our present struggle for independence, she fears that her efforts for the success of our cause have been rather selfish at last. It would give Southern women no pride or pleasure to be exalted to any position, if their brave countrymen were made bondmen and slaves; for them, for their honor and happiness, we live, and the chains of tyranny that fettered their limbs, would also binds us in a slavish thraldom. The moon can only borrow its light from the resplendent beams of the sun; if the regal oak is prostrated in the depth of the forest, the ivy that clings to its strength and embrace will also fall in the ruin—and if our countrymen are degraded and made slaves, Southern women must bid farewell to their proud and high prerogatives of birth add position, and also to their dearest happiness—loving, and being beloved and respected by men who, disdaining the bonds that would enslave them, can still tread the blood-stained soil of the South with their honor untarnished, and a spirit that can never succumb to the tyranny of oppression.

In conclusion please also accept the thanks of the Committee for the kind wishes expressed for the success of the humane enterprise in which we are engaged. The assurance of them will much encourage us to persevere, and among the personal records of the "Home," we will ever point with grateful pleasure to the names of the true and noble editorial gentlemen of the South, who could not turn away from an appeal made in the name, and in the behalf of woman.

MISS M. LOUISE ROGERS,
Corresponding Secretary in behalf of Committee.

HOME FOR INVALID LADIES.

We give here in a condensed form as possible, the plan of the enterprise, and we will be under many obligations if the gentlemen of the press will publish it in their journals until it is known to the public, at the same time hoping they will "say a word for us" as they deem proper and necessary.

The book, to be entitled "Moral Beauties from the Heart of Woman, or Voices from the South," will be published as soon as the blockade is raised. Its contents are contributed by the most distinguished lady writers of the South, to aid in the erection of the Home for invalid Ladies, and the manuscript is now in the hands of Dr. T. S. Powell. One of the most eminent lady writers has been engaged to edit the book; the proof sheets will be printed here, corrected and perfected, so that when the blockade is raised the work will be published at once. Its contents will be choice and miscellaneous literature, written expressly for this work, with a short biography of each contributor. The price of the first quality binding, octavo size, with steel portraits of many of the writers, five dollars; the second quality, bound in muslin, three dollars and a half; the cheapest quality two dollars.

The Home for Invalid Ladies is not designed simply as a hospital or infirmary, but a complete pleasant, and beautiful retreat for invalid ladies of respectability—stately, elegant and commodious. The interior is to be furnished with all necessary medical apparatus, baths, and other appliances; a library of choice reading, musical instruments, and paintings to adorn the walls, while the grounds will be ornamented with stately trees and flowering shrubs, and riding facilities furnished by the inmates. Such healthful accessories, together with the best medical attendance, cannot fail to restore the bloom to the pallid cheek, and bring back elasticity to the faltering step and wasted form of the invalid. The "Home" will be built on a beautiful eminence near the Mineral Spring near this city, the waters of which have been tested as highly beneficial in many diseases.

But while Dr. Powell, by the sale of the book, and his own means, will erect the building, the ladies desire to *furnish* it by donations from all ladies throughout the Confederacy, who will give one dollar or more, and will be glad to have any contributions from gentlhmen who wish success to the enterprise. It will require a considerable amount of money to furnish the home as is desired, but we know there is enough wealth and generosity among the Southern people to accomplish this if they will only promptly respond to the call. The ladies of the North built a similar institution some years ago, and as the superior valor of our troops has been fully tested during the war, Southern women will surely not prove themselves inferior in generosity and benevolence towards their own sex to the women of the Northern States. The name of every donor and the amount given will be promptly recorded, and at a suitable time will be published in pamphlet form, circulated through the country, and permanently kept in the institution. This donation fund will be given to Dr. Powell to make the purchases in Europe that cannot be obtained here. He will report to the Committee of ladies the amount of money received and expended, and this will be published. After the "Home" is completed, he pledges himself to return this donation fund in gratuitous medical attendance upon needy invalid ladies, so while this amount will furnish the "Home," it will also be the means of restoring many a poor woman to health, who might otherwise find death a welcome release from her sufferings.

As the building will be erected as soon as possible, it is earnestly desired to have this donation fund collected at once, so that soon as needed, there may be no delay in its appropriation. Let all who can, and will aid us, do so immediately. We do not say that if the enterprise fails the money will be refunded; for it can, and must succeed, and be completed at the earliest possible time. Nothing need prevent it, but the want of generosity and humanity among the Southern people.

All subscriptions for the book must be forwarded to Dr. Powell, Atlanta, Ga., but donations for the Home, to Mrs. J. N. Simmons, of the same place; and please let the names, post-office and State of all subscribers or donation be plainly and fully stated. If any one wishes to send six dollars, five for the book, and one as a donation, please state it so.

If any gentleman of the press who were not present at the Convention are disposed to assist us in this enterprise, we will be under many obligations if they will copy this circular. The Home for Invalid Ladies is not for the benefit of one State, but for the entire limits of the Confederacy.

Since the above was written, it has been suggested by an influential merchant friend, that perhaps there are numbers of this class—traders and merchants throughout the Confederacy, who would like to give something from their articles of commerce as a donation to the "Home," instead of the money. We will be grateful for anything of the kind, and any merchants who are willing to aid us in this way, if they will send their contributions to the following named gentlemen, they will be sold at the market price, and the money sent to us, or if not sold, the commodities may be shipped to Salmons & Simmons, of Atlanta, Ga., and the amount which each article brings will be credited to the generous donor.

Each person donating twenty dollars or more shall receive, when published, one copy of the work entitled, "*Moral Beauties from the Heart of Woman*," worth ten dollars, and credited with a donation of the amount received, deducting ten dollars for the book.

LIST OF AGENTS.

Mr. J. F. Fears, Macon, Ga.; Messrs. Habersham & Son, Savannah, Ga.; Messrs. Hull & Duck, Columbus, Ga.; Messrs. J. A. Ansley & Co., Augusta, Ga., Mr. F. M. Lucas, Athens, Ga.; Mr. R. F. Hargrove, Rome, Ga.; Mr. James Turner, La-Grange, Ga.; Mr. J. Marshall, Madison, Ga.; Mr. Thomas Harwell, Eatonton, Ga.; Messrs. Newton & Mickleberry, Griffin, Ga.; Messrs. Salmons & Simmons, Atlanta, Ga.; Mr. T. M. Furlow, Americus, Ga.; Messrs. G. W. Williams & Co.; Charleston, S. C.; Mr. John C. Dial, Columbia, S. C.; Mr. P. F Prescud, Raleigh, N. C.; Messrs. J. R. Blossom & Co., Wilmington, N. C.; Messrs. J. R. Branch & Bros. Petersburg, Va.; Messrs. Davis, Roper & Co.; Petersburg, Va.; Messrs. Samuel Ayers & Son, Richmond, Va.; Messrs. Charles T. Worsham & Co., Richmond, Va.; Messrs. McCorkle, Son & Co., Lynchburg, Va.; Messrs. McDaniel & Irby, Lychburg, Va.; Mr. H. L. Johnson, Bristol, Tenn.; Messrs. Clark & Mayo, Knoxville, Tenn.; Mr. John L. M. French, Chattanooga, Tenn.; Messrs. W. B. & A. R. Bell, Montgomery, Ala.; Col. J. R. Powell, Montgomery, Ala.; Messrs. Baker & Lawler, Mobile, Ala.; Messrs. Tarleton & Whiting, Mobile, Ala.; Mr. F. L. Johnson, Selma Ala.; Mr. J. G. L. Hewey, Talladega, Ala.; Mr. J. C. Bradley, Huntsville, Ala.; Messrs. Houghton, Allen & Co., Wetumpka, Ala.; Mr. T. S. Burnett, Greenville, Ala.; Messrs. Allen Ligon & Co., Jackson, Miss.; Messrs. Baskerville & Whitfield, Colum-

bus, Miss.; Messrs. Moody, Ferrall & Co., Enterprise, Miss.
MRS. J. N. SIMMONS,
Chairman, Finance Committee.
M. LOUISE ROGERS, Corresponding Secretary.

THE WORTH OF WOMAN.

FROM THE GERMAN OF SCHILLER.

Honored be woman! she beams on the sight,
Graceful and fair, like a being of light;
Scatters around her wherever she strays,
Roses of bliss on our thorn-covered ways;
Roses of Paradise sent from above,
To be gathered and twined in a garland of Love.

    Man, on passion's stormy ocean,
      Tossed by surges mountain high,
    Courts the hurricane's commotion,
      Spurns at reason's feeble cry,
    Loud the tempest roars around him,
      Louder still it roars within,
    Flashing lights of hope confound him,
      Stun with life's incessant din.

Woman invites him with bliss in her smile,
To cease from his toil and be happy a while;
Whispering wooingly—come to my bower—
Go not in search of the phantom of power—
Honor and wealth are illusory—come!
Happiness dwells in the temples of home.

    Man, with fury stern and savage,
      Prosecutes his brother man,
    Reckless if he bless or ravage,
      Action, action—still his plan.
    Now creating, now destroying,
      Careless wishes tear his breast;
    Ever seeking—ne'er enjoying;
      Still to be, but never blest.

Woman, contented in silent repose,
Enjoys in its beauty life's flower as it blows,
And waters and tends it with innocent heart,
Far richer than man with his treasures of art;
And wiser by far in the circles confined,
Than he with his silence and the lights of the mind.

    Coldly to himself sufficing.
      Man disdains the gentler arts,
    Knoweth not the bliss arising
      From the interchange of hearts.
    Slowly through his bosom stealing,
      Flows the genial current on,
    Till by age's frost congealing
      It is hardened into stone.

> She like the harp that instinctively rings,
> As the night-breathing zephyr soft sighs on the strings,
> Responds to each impulse with steady reply,
> Whether sorrow or pleasure her sympathy try;
> And tear drops and smiles on her countenance play,
> Like sunshine and showers of a morning in May.
>
> Through the range of man's dominion,
> Terror is the ruling word—
> And the standard of opinion
> Is the temper of the sword.
> Strife exults, and pity blushing,
> From the scene departing flies,
> Where the battle madly rushing,
> Brother upon brother dies.
>
> Woman commands with a milder control—
> She rules by enchantment the realms of the soul;
> As she glances around in the light of her smile,
> The war of her passions is hushed for a while,
> And discord, content from his fury to cease,
> Reposes entranced on the pillows of peace.

MAN AND WOMAN.

Man is strong—woman is beautiful. Man is daring in conduct—woman diffident and unassuming. Man shines abroad—woman at home. Man talks to convince—woman to persuade and please. Man has a rugged heart—woman a soft and tender one. Man prevents misery—woman relieves it. Man has science—woman taste. Man has judgment—woman sensibility. Man is a being of justice—woman of mercy.

THE WOMEN OF THE WEST.

Our informant, who gave us the facts in regard to the capture of the Queen of the West, on Red River, and who was forced to go with the Queen down the Atchafalaya, relates the following incident:

At one of the places burnt by the Queen, and owned by a lady who had been thus villainously left houseless, the valiant commander attempted to converse with her on the bank from the deck of his boat. She proved true pluck for him. He asked her:

"Madam, have you a father, brothers or any other relatives in this war?"

The lady was quite young, a widow, with two young boys of five and seven years of age by her side. She answered, in sight of the smouldering ruins of her home:

"I have two brothers in the army, and if you keep on this war twelve years longer, (pressing the heads of her boys,) I shall have *two sons to fight you till their death!* I expect nothing better than murder and arson from any of your tribe."

The commander sloped to his gun-room, while the lady and boys cheered the departure of the Queen of the West the "Bonnie Blue Flag."—*Natchez Courier.*

ATROCITIES OF LINCOLN'S OFFICIALS.

The "Christian Observer" publishes the appended extract of a letter from a clergyman in the country, dated February 21st, 1863:

"I returned yesterday from Stafford, where I had been called to attend a funeral. It was within a mile or two of the Yankee lines. It is the impression that a portion of their army is leaving this region. Their destination is not known. I have buried in this region three females of the highest social position, whose deaths have been caused by Yankee atrocities. They were all in that situation which usually excites our tenderest sympathies. The last one that I buried was the wife of a physician, whose husband was arrested while attending a very sick patient, and kept from his family fourteen days. When he was absent, some of the Yankees, with satanic malignity, came to his wife and told her that they had shot her husband. The shock which this false intelligence produced was more than her delicate frame could bear, and she sank under it. I could tell you much more, but in order to get this off I must close."

Constitutionalist, March 1863.

THE LADIES MAKING SHOES.

The Franklin "Louisianian" says: Quite a number of ladies of this parish have commenced making their own and their children's shoes, and they do very good work. We have seen several pairs of these home-made shoes, and they are not only strong, but they are well proportioned. The cheapest way that they make them is to take the soles of old shoes, soak them in water until they are limber, pick out the old stitches, fit them to the last after the cloth is fitted to the same, sew the soles to the cloth with strong waxed thread, and then turn the shoe, nail the heel to its place, and the shoe is done. It is a cheap, serviceable, and very good cloth shoe.

THE LADIES AND GEN. PRICE—PRESENTATION TO GEN. PRICE.

MONTGOMERY, ALA., Feb. 24, 1863.

Major General Sterling Price: The ladies of Montgomery, fully appreciating your heroic conduct, sublime devotion and invaluable services in the hallowed cause of Southern independence, and desiring to express their high esteem, their earnest undying gratitude to one whose pure patriotism, whose noble self-abnegation, has won the love and admiration of his countrymen and women, beg your acceptance of the accompanying hat, as a very slight testimonial of the regard and confidence of those whose prayers will ever follow you and the gallant men of your command, of whom our national annalist must proclaim—

"Enough of merit has each honored name,
To shine untarnished on the roll of fame,
To stand the example of each distant age,
And add new lustre to the historic page."

Very truly yours,

Mrs. S. E. Given,   Mrs. E. J. Fitzpatrick,
Mrs. W. B. Gilmer, Mrs. E. D. Fagara,
Mrs. E. E. Green,   Mrs. General Fair,
Mrs. Tom Judge,   Mrs. W. Marks,
Mrs. Judge Phelan, Mrs. C. T. Pollard.

Jackson, Miss., March 6, 1863.

Madam: I have the honor to acknowledge the reception, at the hands of Dr. Blackburn, of the elegant "chapeau" sent to me by yourself and other ladies of Montgomery. I accept it with pride, and shall wear it in grateful rememberance of the fair donors.

When the history of this revolution shall be written, I trust that the ladies of the South may receive that credit to which their lofty and self-sacrificing patriotism so justly entitles them. Through our darkest hours they have stood firm and unshaken, seeing, with the eye of faith the rainbow of promise spanning the horizon of the future, when to others all seemed gloomy, desolate and hopeless. The first to counsel resistance to tyranny, they have nobly maintained their position by sending forth to battle, and perhaps to death, the objects of their earthly adoration; and this not reluctantly, as the miser parts with his gold, but cheerfully and courageously they have laid their temporal happiness on the altar of their country, content to lose everything save honor, and determined that at any hazard it should be maintained. Nor have their exertions stopped here. The soldiers of every battle-field, and on every starving march, and in every hospital, have been nerved, strengthened and encouraged by the words of cheer and sympathy that have reached them from home. Nobly have the women of the South fulfilled their mission in this our struggle for constitutional government. Their conduct gives assurance to the world that men descended from such mothers, having such wives and sisters, can never be made to bow the neck to the yoke of oppression, no matter with what strength it may be forced upon them.

For the complimentary expressions toward myself, contained in your letter, I am deeply grateful, but I cannot accept them without assuring you that whatever of good to the cause I may have been enabled to accomplish is due to the exertions of the noble men who have constituted my command. They have endured the heats of summer and colds of winter—have faced death in its most horrid forms, in camp and on the battle field, with a sublime heroism to which history presents few parallels. Again thanking you for your kind remembrance of me, I remain, very respectfully, your friend and obedient servant,
STERLING PRICE, Major General.
Mrs. Alex. F. Givens and others, Montgomery, Alabama.

THE GREATEST ATROCITY YET OF THE ENEMY.

Mr. Caswell Woods, a resident of Craven county, North Carolina, had his house entered at midnight on the second of October by two Yankee troopers armed with pistol and sabre, who committed outrages of which the details are not fit for publication. Mr. Woods is represented to be a respectable citizen. The Richmond "Enquirer" gives the main facts of the case as contained in the subjoined depositions by Mr. Woods and his wife. It is with reluctance that we insert details so shocking to all sense of delicacy, but the necessity of placing on record such atrocities as exhibit the character of our foe who permits their perpetration, requires this duty of us. Mr. Woods deposes as follows:

"I came down stairs in my night clothes. The front door had been burst open. One of the men had rode into the house on his horse. The other walked in. The one on the horse, who appeared to be an officer, commenced cursing me, and asked me where I was two days before. When I told him I was home, he said, 'You lie, for you shot at me.' Upon this pretence, they cut the cord from a bed in the room, said they would hang him, but finally tied him, took him out of the house and lashed him to a tree, with the threat of instant death if he made any outcry or attempted to get loose. They returned to the house and locked the door after them, and the old man had the inexpressible agony of listening for the rest of the night to the screams and doleful lamentations of his wife and daughter."

The statement made by Mrs. Woods in her deposition of what passed inside, is truly heartrending. The unparalleled villians made the poor helpless women not merely the victims of their brutal lust, but accompanied the outrage, which is worse than death, with circumstances that mark them as the most abandoned of villians. With pistol in hand and with threat of instant death, the deponent was required by one of the beasts to divest herself of every particle of clothing. But this was almost Christian treatment compared with other acts which may not be related. While such were her own sufferings, the shrieks of her daughter in another room told that hers was a similar fate. About sunrise the next morning the human devils departed.

The following remarks were made by the "Enquirer" on the subject;

The depositions have been laid before us with the suggestion endorsed thereon by the Adjutant General "that so much of this account as is not too foul for publication should be given to the public, through the press, in order that the righteous indignation of our people, our Generals and our armies, may, under the providence of God, visit a just retribution upon an enemy so fiendlike." Concurring in the propriety of the suggestion, we have acted accordingly.

We are happy to say that General Gustavus W. Smith has directed every effort to be made to ascertain the names of the parties, and to "demand their delivery for trial and punishment." We hope copies of the depositions have been forwarded to the authorities of the enemy. Surely there are some, even among them, who would be horrified by such conduct. The vengeance of Heaven must light upon them and their cause!

January 6, 1863.

ROBBERY OF A LADY.

We learn from the Memphis "Argus" that during General Hovey's late expedition into this State, a lot of soldiers went to the plantation of a Miss Hill, on Coldwater, twenty-two miles from Friar's Point, in Coahoma county, and ransacked her premises, taking from her $30,000 in gold, and a large lot of Confederate scrip; also sixty mules, and much other property. Miss Hill's father died a few weeks ago, and had left her an immense estate, which has been taken from her in a single day. There was no white male person on the premises when the stragglers 'entered, but one man, the overseer, who ranaway at lightning speed.

Miss H. went to Helena, accompanied by her guardian, on the 13th, to endeavor to recover her property, when she received only fair promises from the Federal commander. No clue was obtained as to the whereabouts of her property.

Memphis Appeal, Dec. 22.

PATRIOTIC AND TRUE DEVOTION OF WOMAN.

The following is an extract from a recent letter from Mrs. M. L. Woodson, now residing in Texas, to her sister, Mrs. Isaac Winship, the indefatigable and patriotic President of the Atlanta Hospital Association. We doubt not that the sentiments will meet a hearty response from the noble self-sacrificing women of the whole South:

My Dear Sister: * * *. I have nothing to communicate at present. You have seen in the papers the account of the fall of Arkansas Post. My two poor boys were there, but where they *are now* I do not know. We learned from a Commissary who made his escape from the Post, that they were in the fight.— Miller was in charge of a hospital, but he left it and went into the trenches and fought as a private. The returned soldier says he saw Swan and Miller both as they went into the fight, but knows no more concerning them. They were three days and nights in the trenches, without sleep, and I expect without food. Judging from the reports we have, they must have suffered awfully from sickness while at the Post. The company which went from here lost a great many by sickness.

There were 8,000 men at the Post, and only 4,400 were reported as able to go into the battle. They fought seven gunboats and the land force, said to be 40,000 strong, for thirty-six hours. Being completely surrounded by land forces, the few who escaped, did so by swimming.

Swan had just recovered from a spell of six weeks' illness, and returned to camps. Not a line from anybody at that place has ever reached us since the battle. The sick were left in the hospitals. Some of my nearest neighbors were there, but their friends have not heard from them, nor do we know who were among the killed and wounded. We know but little besides what the newspapers say.

If my sons *are alive*, they are prisoners, and taken to some Lincoln prison. The reflection that they are in the hands of such cruel, inhumane creatures is as much as I have fortitude and patriotism to bear. But they are in the hands of God, and to him I commit them, but if they return to me no more, my setting sun will go down in clouds. Yet I will not despair— our cause is worthy of any sacrifice—even the loss of my beloved and brave boys will not dampen my zeal in my country's cause—No; better a thousand times, that every Southern man should perish, than yield their cause. All have suffered the loss, either of kindred or friends, in this cruel war, and I must not complain if it is my fate to have torn from me those I loved with no common affection; and no mother had more cause to love her sons and cherish their memory. Mine were brave and honorable men, and warm-hearted and affectionate to me and each other, and when all were around me no happier mother could be found on earth. But it is a desolate home now, and perhaps may ever remain so.

I have other children to raise, and my duty to them will prevent indulgence in useless repining. So if the worst comes, I shall submit, with patience, to the will of Heaven, and discharge the duty I owe to others; but if I lose my dear boys life will lose its charms to me, though I shall love my country none the less. On my country's freedom I have set my heart, on her altars I have placed my sons and my hopes.

I would not see my children made slaves, or my country subjugated by a hated foe. No, rather let their young lives be offered up, and their mother go broken hearted to the grave.

But the arm of God is not shortened, that he cannot save even those in the enemy's hands; so I will still entertain some hope for the safe return of my dear boys.   *   *   *.   *

Your sister,   M. L. WOODSON.

Intelligencer, April, 1863;·

STARTLING REVELATIONS BY A MISSOURIAN WHO WAS TO HAVE BEEN HUNG BY THE YANKEES.

The "Mississippian" contains a letter written by a soldier of the Missouri army, who was captured and charged with being a spy. He had frequent interviews with the officers high in command, and so certain were they of hanging him that they spoke quite unreservedly of their intentions and feelings toward the South. The following is an extract:

From the point of my capture, I made with the entire Federal army a march of about one hundred miles, during which march my opportunities and frequent conversations with some of the leading men, afforded me good grounds for knowing and judging of the feelings and intentions of those constituting the Western Department. And I know to a certainty that we must work to save ourselves from a worse fate than has yet been felt by any. The enemy's present design is to re-open the Mississippi river, and while establishing communication between two of ther departments, cut off communication between two of ours, thus leaving all the West without arms and at their mercy, and for this purpose they will use all the force both here and west of the Mississippi. And even now. they are massing rapidly at the principle points by Nashville, Corinth, Memphis, Helena, and Columbus, Kentucky. Further it was asserted to me by reliable (or at least influential) men as Gen. Rosecrans and McCook, that if they ever came South again they would not leave a house or field, man, woman, child or dog. So let us at once prepare, for we will have work to do this winter; let one and all throw aside all idea that there is to be anything hoped for from foreign powers or Democratic victories, or any other Yankee humbug.

THE TEN MISSOURI MURDERS.

The ten Confederate soldiers whom the Abolition brute, McNeill, lately murdered in Missouri, were not executed for killing an enemy. It seems that a man was missing from the neighborhood of the ten, and they were held responsible for his safety, and ordered to have him forthcoming within a fixed time, under the penalty of death. The time passed, and they were slain. It now turns out that the day after the murder the missing man returned to his home. He had not been molested, and was absent on business which he did not desire to communicate to his friends. This statement is made on the authority of a St. Louis paper. The crime in the case is made more terrible by this statement.

ATROCIOUS MURDER BY YANKEES IN MISSOURI.

The Little Rock (Arkansas) "Democrat," publishes the following:

VAN BUREN, August 20, 1862.

R. H. JOHNSON, ESQ.—*Dear Sir:* The enclosed letter from Mrs. Dunn to her husband's brother, informing him of the murder of her husband by a party of Missouri militia, you will find of sufficient interest for publication. William and James H. Dunn were beef contractors in Price's army and gentlemen of high standing.

Respectfully, yours, WM. WALKER.

JUNE 25th, 1862.

To MR. J. H. DUNN—*Dear Brother:* I have bad news to communicate to you. Poor William came home Saturday evening—Johnson and Clay were here when he came home. He had not been here more than a half hour when he went to put away his horse—Johnson and Clay went with him. He had just got his saddle off, when forty or fifty of the State militia came galloping up, and were at the barn gate before they saw them. William and Clay ran into the orchard, and William lay down behind the bushes by the fence; they followed and took Clay prisoner; they fired at William twice, but missed him; he then raised up, came out and told them to take him. They questioned him about what he had been doing and he told them he had just come home from Coffee's camp—they said he had come to get news for Coffee, and they would kill him. They took him over the orchard and pasture fences through the woods to hunt Johnson and his horse, which, of course, he knew nothing about, but they got his horse. They then brought William around to the south gate. He asked them if he might come to the house to see his wife and children, but they cursed him and told him no, so he called me out there and whispered to me to go to the house and empty the pockets of his coat and bring it to him; I did so, and then he told me, "Annie these men are going to kill me, I must bid you good bye, I want you to take care of the children, and do the best you can; Jim will help you raise my children." He then asked me to bring Frank to see him, the Lieutenant told him to hurry, I went to the house to get Frank who was asleep and had not yet seen his father since he came home. The Lieutenant called William out across the road and told him he should shoot him there and to get through his talk quick. William came back and told mother and me that they were going to kill him right there, but mother and I threw ourselves on him and told them they must kill us first. They ordered us off or they would shoot us, and I think they would have shot us; they then told William to get on his horse, he did so, and took Frank to his arms and bid him good bye, that those men were going to kill his father. Frank cried and screamed, and said, men don't kill my pa! and I told them to look at those two little helpless children and then tell me if they could have the heart to kill my husband, but they only cursed and mocked us; but told us they would not hurt him, only take him with them. So they started down the country road towards Fidelity; then after going about a quarter of a mile they stopped, (so Clay says) made him get off his horse, and took him through the woods down a hollow to the left hand and there by a big tree shot him with six balls. We heard the firing and followed—I found him on his knee; with his poor face in a pool of blood; I called him and thought he answered, but no, his lips were sealed in death. He was shot twice in the head, three times in the left arm and once in the left side. We laid him to rest by his father's side in the grave yard, at the meeting house. He looked very natural—he must have died instantly, Jimmy try to bear it the best you can, it is a severe affliction to us all. I don't want you to come home, stay away until you know it is safe to come, or you may share the same fate. Mother says she wants us to be together now, there are so few of us; but she is afraid to go south at this season of the year. Whas do you think it advisable for us to do?

The same crowd of State milltia under Lieut. Lefevre, passed here yesterday (Monday) going back to Mount Vernon. The Union men, Andy Foster, the Motley's Willoughbys, Smiths and Oliver, that came in with the State militia Saturday as soon as they heard what had happened, that night without waiting to cut their wheat, they were afraid to stay. Jimmy, on no account attempt to come home, but as soon as you think it best, we will come to you, if we are spared.

Clay says, after they had killed him, Lieutenant Lefevre rode among his men asking who would have his hat; none would take it, so he threw it and his coat to Clay, and told him damn him, take them and go take care of that man. We met Clay bringing his hat and coat, and he turned back with us to search for William.

I want you to let the Southern men read of this cold blooded

murder. We are going to try and get Mr. May to go and see you. From your afflicted sister-in-law,
ANNIE C. DUNN.

INCIDENTS OF THE BATTLE OF FREDERICKSBURG—THE PEOPLE OF THE TOWN WHO REMAINED—THE WOMEN.

The Yankee Generals were almost thunderstruck at finding so many persons through a shelling lasting twelve hours, and carried on without intermission, with one hundred and forty-three guns. Gen. Sturgis told a lady that the women of Fredericksburg ought to be handed down to the latest posterity as model heroines. He then said to the same lady—"madam, it is too dangerous for you to remain longer, General Lee will shell the town; go over to the other side, I will insure you protection and a return whenever you choose to come back." The lady's reply was quite significant—"No sir," said she, "I have no more business across that river than a Yankee has in Heaven; I shall stay and take the best care I can of my property." He then asked if she had a husband in the Southern army. "No, sir, I have a son; but if my husband does not now enlist and avenge the vandalism you have committed on my town and its people, I shall get a divorce." Said Sturgis, "I admire your pluck, madam, and from this time forward, as long as I remain, you shall be protected."

In another instance, a gentleman had been arrested, and was being carried before an officer, when his daughter, one of the most beautiful and accomplished girls in the city, seized an old sword lying near, and following the guard, who was conducting her father, and who was abusing him, bade him desist, threatening him with instant death if he should harm her father, accompanied him to the presence of the officer, when both were released. A Yankee officer who witnessed this scene said he would rather fight the best regiment of the South than encounter the women of Fredericksburg.

THE FIDELITY OF THE SLAVES.

One of the most gratifying of the many interesting incidents of the occupation of Fredericksburg was the faithful conduct of the slaves who remained. In several instances they saved, amid the perfect rain of shot and shell, houses and indeed squares from destruction. In other instances, they claimed and secured protection for the property of their owners, whilst in not a few instances they asked to be permitted to share the plunder with the thieving soldiery, and getting the permission, took care to save for those who had left, many valuable articles.

YANKEE LETTERS—WHAT THEY SAY.

I have been permitted to read or rather to glance at a large number of letters written by the home people to their friends in the field.

They all complain of the great scarcity of labor, representing that the crops in many instances, could not be harvested for the want of it. They express strong hopes of speedy peace, and say that it is folly to expect ever to raise another army in the North. One girl says she dispairs of ever getting a husband, as there is not a decent, marriageable man within twenty miles of her.

MORE VANDALISM.

The Yankees have committed so many abominable wickednesses, that it will hardly be credited when it is told that they destroyed the Masonic regalia, carried off the charters of the lodges, and actually burnt some of the Bibles found in private houses and churches. As one of the *ruses* resorted to in facilitating their thieving operations, they would go to the houses which were tenanted, arrest its occupants, and carry them across the river. Whilst this was going on, another party would enter the houses, bearing off and destroying whatever they might find.

POISONED BULLETS.

I have seen, to-day some of these horrid looking messengers. They are made in three parts, and so constructed that upon entering the body, the head separates from the rest of the bullet, which is drawn forward, the hindmost part remaining at the point of entrance, and causing the wound to fester, and as a sure consequence, it is said, death must ensue.

Correspondence of the Richmond Enquirer.

A CONFEDERATE ALPHABET.

A is for Anderson, foremost and least,
B is for Bethel, or Butler the Beast;
C is for Chase and also for Cheat,
D is for Darkies, Disaster, Defeat;
E is for Eagle, transformed to a crow,
F is the Flag spreading ruin and woe;
G is for Gibbet on which we will hang,
Hunter the Hound and all of his gang;
I is the infamy of which they are proud,
J Johnson the Jackall, the worst of the crowd;
K is the Kalendar of accidents dire,
L is for Lincoln the Long Legged Liar;
M's for McClellan who Richmond would see,
N is for Never, when his it shall be;
O shows what Yankees will make by the war,
Q is for Query, "what is it all for?"
P, which was passed, stands for Puppy and Pope,
R is for Rosecrans, Rascal and Rope;

S stands for Seward, well surnamed the Snake,
T, the three months, the Rebellion will take;
U's for the Union of all that is base,
V for the Victories that never took place;
W for Winfield, whose victories great,
Xerxes-like ended in shameful defeat;
Y stands for Yankees that self-esteemed nation,
Z is for Zero, their true valuation.
Chattanooga Rebel.

NORTHERN VIRTUE.

The Petersburg "Express," after giving specimens from a Yankee love letter picked up on a battle field, says:

Of all the Yankee letters we have read since the commencement of this war, whether written by maidens, wives, husbands or lovers, we have not yet seen one that would bear a virtuous criticism. They are filled with such obscene reference and depraved avowals, that a virtuous man or woman must blush in reading them, to think of the nature of the people in whom we have so long associated on equal terms.

UNION SENTIMENT IN NEW ORLEANS.

A Yankee letter-writer gives the following illustrations of the presence of a Union sentiment in New Orleans city, in which the Northern papers have been indulging so largely:

"The Union feeling existing there—that they talk so much about—does not exist; for Butler says that even the women and children are the ' d—d'st rebels ' he ever saw, and there has been but little Union feeling displayed where there was nothing to be gained. Self-interest has been the parent of all Union feeling exhibited there; of this I feel certain. To demonstrate this fact, let me relate an incident which I know to be authentic. A Mrs. ———, whose husband has come out strong on the Union subject, knowing that in the public schools there would be many opportunities for those who would hurrah for the stars and stripes, and desiring to obtain the principalship of one of the girls' high schools, called upon Gen. Butler, accompanied by a ' secesh ' lady, who was anxious to see the brute without having any business herself to take here there. Mrs. ———, after complimenting Butler highly upon the condition of the streets, and the city generally, and expressing her devoted allegiance to the old flag, stated that she called, actuated solely by the promptings of her heart, to take the oath of allegiance. Butler allowed her to get that far, and no farther. ' Get out, madam! get out! don't say another word. I have never seen the woman in the South yet who would take the oath of allegiance, or even hear of it, unless they had an object to gain in it. They are the damndest rebels in the whole Confederacy of rebels. Get out, madam; you want some favor under me; go.' And out she had to go. The secesh lady couldn't keep it, you may be sure; and it was no time before the story was out. Another incident: While our vessel way lying at the pickets, the Yankee sentinels picked up a little boy of about six years, who was playing near them, and tried to induce him to hurrah for Lincoln. 'I won't.' 'Hurrah, and I'll give you something.' 'I won't.' Catching him up, and suspending the little fellow over the canal, they said: 'Hurrah for Lincoln, or we'll drop you in.' 'Drop and be damned,' said the little rebel; and, with a shout, they set him down, saying he was rebel pluck to the backbone. These two instances that I know of, are pretty fair specimens of the Union feeling there."

THE GREATEST BATTLE.

The more we view it and familiarize ourselves with its details, the more clearly the fact stands out that the battle of Sharpsburg, or Antietam, was, on our part, the greatest engagement of modern times. Our correspondent's declaration, that we fought 40,000 against a force of 125,000, is sustained by Gen. Lee in his address to the army. That so small a force, ragged, bare-foot, half-starved and worn down by a long series of battles and severe marches, should have proved a full match for three times their number of fresh and well disciplined Yankees, is indeed a marvel. History will so record it, and it will stand out for all time as incontestible proof of our superiority over the North in all that goes to make up a brave and warlike people.

And again: the fact that our army has remained for weeks within a few miles of McClellan, without his venturing to attack us, is evidence that his forces were so badly crippled in the fight that they have been totally unable to renew it.

Savannah Republican.

GEN. LEE'S ADDRESS TO HIS ARMY.

General Lee has issued the following address to his soldiers. He recounts their achievements with eloquence, and delivers to them the thanks of the President, and bestows, in feeling terms, the praise they have so well earned:

HEADQUARTERS ARMY OF NORTHERN VIRGINIA, }
October 2, 1862. }

General Orders, No. 116.

In reviewing the achievements of the Army during the present campaign, the Commanding General cannot withhold the expression of his admiration of the indomitable courage it has displayed in battle, and its cheerful endurance of privation and hardship on the march.

Since your great victories around Richmond you have defeated the enemy at Cedar mountain, expelled him from the Rappahannock, and, after a conflict of three days, utterly repulsed him on the Plains of Manassas, and forced him to take shelter within the fortifications around the capital.

Without halting for repose you crossed the Potomac, stormed the heights of Harper's Ferry, made prisoners of more than eleven thousand men, and captured upwards of seventy pieces of artillery, all their small arms and other munitions of war.

While one corps of the army was thus engaged, the other insured its success by arresting at Boonsboro' the combined armies of the enemy, advancing under their favorite general, to the relief of their beleaguered comrades.

On the field of Sharpsburg, with less than one-third his number, you resisted, from daylight until dark, the whole army of the enemy, and repulsed every attack along his entire front, of more than four miles in extent.

The whole of the following day you stood prepared to resume the conflict on the same ground, and retired next morning, without molestation, across the Potomac.

Two attempts subsequently made by the enemy to follow you across the river, have resulted in his complete discomfiture, and being driven back with loss.

Achievements such as these demanded much valor and patriotism. History records few examples of greater fortitude and endurance than this army has exhibited; and I am commissioned by the President to thank you in the name of the Confederate States for the undying fame you have won for their arms.

Much as you have done, much more remains to be accomplished. The enemy again threatens us with invasion, and to your tried valor and patriotism, the country looks with confidence for deliverance and safety; your past exploits give assurance that this confidence is not misplaced.

R. E. LEE, General Commanding.

FIRST NAVAL VICTORY IN VIRGINIA—HISTORY OF THE MERIMAC AND HER COMMANDER, ADMIRAL FRANKLIN BUCHANAN.

This distinguished naval officer is a native of the State of Maryland, but for some years resided in Pennsylvania, from which State he was appointed a midshipman. He entered the navy on the 28th of January, 1815, and continued, in various positions, until the 14th of September, 1855, when he was made captain. Buchanan was in the United States naval service for forty-five years, twenty-one of which were spent at sea. His last cruise, while in the service of that government, was in command of the steam frigate Susquehanna, on the Japan Expedition in 1855.

On the 19th April, when the Massachusetts troops were attacked on their passage through Baltimore city, Capt. Buchanan was in command of the navy yard at Washington. He immediately resigned his commission, and, in a short time thereafter, tendered his services to the Southern Confederacy, which were promptly accepted, and he drew his sword in defence of Southern independence. He was assigned to duty as Chief of Orders and Detail, in the Confederate navy, then in its infancy, and in February, 1862, hoisted his flag at Norfolk on board the iron-clad frigate Virginia, such, being the name given by the Confederate Navy Department to the United States frigate Merrimac, partially burnt and sunk by Commodore Paulding, when the Federal forces evacuated the Norfolk navy yard on the secession of Virginia, and on Saturday, the 8th of March, 1862, engaged the enemy off Newport's News. It may not be uninteresting to the readers of our paper to give here a short description of this the greatest naval engagement that ever took place in American waters.

The Virginia had been cut loose from her moorings, and was on her way down the harbor, when Commodore Buchanan, calling "all hands to muster," delivered the following brief, but spirited address to the crew:

"Men, the eyes of your country are upon you. You are fighting for your rights—your liberties—your wives and children. You must not be content with only doing your duty; but do *more than your duty!* Those ships (pointing to the Yankee vessels) must be taken, and you shall not complain that I do not take you close enough. Go to your guns!"

How well the officers and the gallant crew of that "monster of the deep" performed their whole duty, we let an eye-witness of that memorable engagement tell:

"The morning was still as that of a Sabbath. The two Yankee frigates lay with their boats at the boom, and wash-clothes in the rigging. Did they see the long, dark hull? Had they made her out? Was it ignorance, apathy, or composure? These were the questions we discussed as we steamed across the flats to the south of the frigates with the two gallant little gunboats well on our starboard beam heading up for the enemy. Our doubts were solved by the heavy boom of a gun from beyond Sewell's Point. The reverberation rolled across the sun-lit water and died away, but still the clothes hung in the rigging, still the boats lay at the booms. Another gun (21 minutes past 1) broke on the air, and a tug started from Newport's News; while at the same time two others left Old Point, taking the channel inside Hampton bar. Steadily, with a grim and ominous silence, the Virginia glides through the water, steadily and with defiant valor the Beaufort and Raleigh followed where she led. At ten minutes to two, a rifle gun from one of these little vessels rang out, then a white puff from her consort. Still the clothes in the rigging, still the boats at the boom? Was this confidence? It could not be ignorance. Did it mean torpedoes, submarine batteries, infernal machines? The gunboats have fired again, and lo! here away to the eastward were the Roanoke and Minnesota rising like prodigious castles above the placid water, the first under steam, the second in tow. Other puffs of smoke, other sharp reports from the gunboats, but the Virginia goes on steadily, silently to do her work. Now the in-shore frigate, the Cumberland, fires; now the Virginia close aboard; now Sewell's Point battery; now the Minnesota; now the Roanoke; now the air trembles with the cannonade. Now the Virginia delivers both broadsides; now she runs full against the Cumberland's starboard bow; now the smoke clears away, and she appears heading up James River. This at twenty-two minutes to two. The Congress now lets fall foretopsail, and then the main, and so with a tug along-side, starts down the north channel, where the Minnesota has grounded, and presently runs plump ashore. Meanwhile the Virginia opens fire upon the Yankee fort, slowly she steams back, and the Cumberland, sunk now to her white-streak, opens upon her again. A gallant man fought that ship—a man worthy to have maintained a better cause. Gun after gun he fired, lower and lower sunk his ship, his last discharge comes from his pivot gun, the ship lurches to starboard, now to port, his flag streams out wildly, and now the Cumberland goes down on her beamends, at once a monument and an epitaph of the gallant man who fought her. The Virginia stops. Is she aground? And the gunboat? Raleigh and Beaufort! glorious Parker! glorious Alexander! there they are on the quarters of the Congress hammering away, and creeping up closer and closer all the time. At ten minutes to four the Congress struck. Parker hauled down the ensign, run up his own battle-flag in its place, there the heroic Taylor, who fought the Fanny at Roanoke Island and Elizabeth City, got his wound—there the gallant young Hutter fell, all shot by the dastards who fired from the ship and shore when the white flag was flying at the main and mizen of the Congress!

"Here too, and in the same way, Flag Officer Buchanan, and Flag Lieut. R. D. Minor, were wounded. Now the James River gunboats, whose dark smoke had been seen against the blue distance ever since 3 o'clock, came dashing along past the shore batteries. Tucker, the courtly and chivalrous, leading the van, with the Jamestown, Lieut. Commanding Barney, close aboard, and the little Teaser, Lieut. Webb, in her wake—like a bow-legged bull dog in chase of the long, lean, stag-hound. It was a gallant dash, and once past the batteries, the two heavy vessels took position in line of battle, while the Teaser dashed at the Minnesota, looking no larger than a cock boat. And right well she maintained the honor of her flag and the appropriateness of her name. Now the Roanoke puts her helm up and declines the battle. Now the Virginia is thundering away again. The Teaser is still closer in. We are closer in—sizz comes a shell ahead, presently another astern, finally a third with a clear, sharp whizz, just over head, to the great delight of the Commodore, who appreciated the compliment of these good shots, which were the last of six shots directed at the Harmony. Now the schooner Reindeer comes foaming along, cut out from under the shore batteries; she reports, and is sent up in charge of acting Master Gibbs.

"And next the gallant Beaufort runs down. Parker steps and brings on board the great piece of bunting we saw hauled down just now. He brings also some thirty prisoners and some wounded men—men wounded under that white flag yonder desecrated by the Yankees. One of these lies stretched out, decently covered over, gasping out his life on the deck—a Yankee shot through the head, all bloody and ghastly, killed by the inhuman fire of his own people. Another pale and stern, the Captain of the Beaufort's gun, lies there too, a noble specimen of a man who has since gone where the weary are at rest. A gallant man, a brave seaman!

"We shake hands with Parker; he gets back to his vessel slightly wounded, as is Alexander, and steams back gallantly to the fight. The Patrick Henry, the Jamestown, the Teaser, the Beaufort, the Raleigh, and the grand old Virginia, are all thundering away. We steam down and speak the first. We hear a report of casualties, we shake hands with friends. we shove off, cheer and steam towards the Swash Channel. Presently through the thickening gloom we see a red glare, it grows larger, and brighter, and redder. It creeps higher and higher, and now gun after gun booming on the still night as the fire reaches them, the batteries of the Congress are discharged across the water in harmless thunder. It was a grand sight to see, and by the light of the burning ship, we made our way back to Norfolk. At half-past eleven the act of retribution was complete, for at that hour, with a great noise, she blew up."

When Commodore Buchanan was wounded and taken below, a feeling of deep sadness pervaded the entire crew, but they soon rallied when Flag Lieutenant Minor, himself wounded and sent below, appeared on deck and delivered to them the following message from the noble flag officer:

"Tell Mr. Jones to fight the ship to the last—tell the men that I am not mortally wounded and hope to be with them again very soon."

The cheers that greeted the delivery of this message resounded far above the cannon's roar, and every man was again quickly at his post, dealing death and destruction with their heavy guns.

Congress was in session when the engagement took place and shortly thereafter passed a bill creating the grade of Admiral in the navy, to which position Buchanan was nominated by the President and confirmed by the Senate.

The news of the great naval victory fled over the country with electric speed, and was received with wonder and astonishment by the people of the South, who regarded it as the turning point in our fortunes, then under a cloud from recent disasters to our arms at Donaldson and other places.

England and France, with all their powerful resources, for two years had been endeavoring to solve the problem of iron-clad ships, but it remained for the Southern Confederacy, the youngest sister in the family of nations, to demonstrate conclusively, by actual trial in battle, their great efficiency, and thus to radically revolutionize the old system of naval warfare, a fact still more wonderful when we consider that the Virginia was cut down, mailed, armed, manned and fought with unprecedented success, all within the brief space of six months, by a people heretofore entirely dependent upon the Yankee States for all commercial advantages.—*Illustrated News.*

THE FIRST NAVAL VICTORY ON THE MISSISSIPPI RIVER, BY GEN. JEFF. THOMPSON.

Reader, you have before you an account of the exploits of the gallant and dashing Thompson, one of the heroes of this war, who shines with the notable refulgence pertaining to each member of that cherished constellation to which we trust we look in the darkest hour of the nation's adversity—a constellation we may term the Orion of our national firmament, which with nerve firm strung and eye unblanched at the fierce menace of the foe, advances and takes the Yankee bull by the horns. The stars in this constellation are household words. The little children are familiar with the name of Ashby, Stuart, Morgan, Forrest and Jeff. Thompson.

He is not very handsome, but, then, his handsome deeds make amends for what he lacks in personal beauty. An English jockey would pronounce him "a rum un to look at, but a good un to go," as in truth he is. That thin face has none of the hatchet about it, but a great deal of the tomahawk. His eye does not gleam with sheet-lightning, but gives forth a forked flash when much excited. A friend who is acquainted with his great powers of physical endurance thinks he is made up of "cat-gut and steel-filings." His address is easy and graceful, his manner genial and earnest, and his utterance as rapid as volleys of musketry, though clear and distinct.

He was born on the 26th of January, 1826, at Harper's Ferry, Virginia. His father, Meriwether Thompson, was born in Hanover county, and his mother, Martha Slaughter Broadus, was born in Culpeper county. He was intended and educated for the army, and from his early youth has manifested a strong passion for the profession of arms. Through political influences he was not admitted to West Point, but he understands the art of war none the less thoroughly on that account, for the reason that his soul has always been bent on the study of warfare and his spirit eager for the fray.

We find him at the age of 17 years selling goods in Charlestown, Virginia; afterwards, in Shepherdstown, Virginia; then in Philadelphia, Pennsylvania; Baltimore, Maryland; and from thence he emigrates to Missouri, in 1847. He continues clerking until the year 1851, when the railroad system of Missouri is inaugurated and he enters the service of the Hannibal and St. Joseph railroad company as engineer, and is placed in charge of the construction of the first division, West. He resigns his position to survey public lands in Kansas and Nebraska, and, after finishing several contracts, commences the real estate brokerage business in St. Joseph, Missouri, which business, interpersed with railroad enterprises, he continues up to the election of Lincoln, at which time he is Mayor of the city of St. Joseph, President of the Rose Port and Marysville railroad, Secretary of the St. Joseph and Topeka railroad, and directly or indirectly connected with every public enterprise in Northwest Missouri. A good many irons for one man to have in the fire, but we have yet to learn that any of them were injured through inattention on his part.

Upon the result of the election being known, he immediately quit all business and attempted to arouse the people of Missouri and other Border States to their true danger, and induce them to take time by the forelock. The first address after the election, issued in a Border States, urging their secession, was, we believe, from his pen. He devoted his attention to the military and reorganized a large number of companies in Northwest Missouri, of which he had been chief officer and inspector for several years. Upon the meeting of the Legislature, he visited Jefferson City and remained during the entire sessions, urging the passage of the "Military Bill" and other schemes which would place Missouri in a state of readiness when the storm should burst upon her. The preparations had just begun, when Blair and Lyon captured Gen. Frost's command at Camp Jackson, St. Louis.

The forces under command of Gen. Thompson, at St. Joseph, prepared to resist any attempt the Federal troops might make toward them, but, by that unfortunate treaty between General Price and Gen. Harney, they were disbanded. He started to Virginia to cast his fortunes with his native State, but upon arriving at Memphis he found Governor Jackson had called the Missourians into the field, and he immediately returned to Missouri. He entered the State in Ripley county, and the next day was elected Lieutenant Colonel of a battalion. In a week he had a regiment, and in two weeks thereafter was elected Brigadier General of twenty-five hundred brave and earnest men. This was on the 25th day of July, 1861, and from that day he commenced harrassing the enemy, and until December 1st, there was scarcely a day that he did not exchange shots with them. During the month of October, he fought at Pattonsville, Big River Bridge, Blackwater Station, Frederickstown and Bloomington. The months of December and January were spent at New Madrid, Missouri, in disbanding the Missouri State Guard, and reorganizing the men as Confederate States troops; yet, in these two months, several excursions broke the monotony of business. The steamboat Platte Valley was captured, the town of Commerce and the steamboat City of Allen felt his presence, and numerous pickets and scouting parties around Bird's Point were compelled to yield their overcoats and arms to his men. He withdrew his men across the swamp before the fall of New Madrid, and when the Western troops were ordered to join Gen. Beauregard, at Corinth, he marched down the Crowley Ridge to Helena, and from thence by boat went to Memphis. He here found that the river defence fleet, known as the "Cotton-boat Fleet," needed gunners and marines, and immediately volunteered his artillery and infantry. They were gladly accepted, and on the 10th of May, above Fort Pillow, he gained the first naval victory on the Mississippi river. There was no little chagrin felt and expressed by naval officers, who had been so long resting on their oars and rusting with inactivity, when a land-lubber from Western plains showed them "some things could be done as well as others." The defeat at Memphis might have turned out a victory, had he and his men been aboard.

After the fall of Memphis, he was placed in charge of the lines around that city, and while in the performance of his duty made several narrow escapes from being captured. From thence he was transferred to Pontchatoula, Louisiana, to watch Beast Butler's movements.

The remoteness of the scene of action on which Gen. Thompson has been engaged since the commencement of the war, has prevented so full an account of his exploits being recorded in the newspapers as of other leaders of his class, whose adventures have figured more conspicuously in the letters of army correspondents. Several battles have been fought in Missouri and the Southwest, besides skirmishes without number, that only find a record in the terse sentences of the official report filed away in the war office. When an authentic history of the Trans-Mississippi campaigns shall be written, the readers, who have had but a vague idea of facts, formed by a stray paragraph, now and then, in the daily press, will be astonished at their magnitude, and the hardships and severe labors of the gallant men who have accomplished wonders with such insignificant means as have been placed at their disposal. In most of these exploits, the subject of our sketch has figured conspicuously and has won for himself the entire confidence of the men who have followed him. With the exception of Gen. Price, there is, perhaps, no man around whom the Missourians would more enthusiastically rally than Jeff. Thompson, if sent among them. We trust, ere many months, his sabre will flash on the plains of Northern Missouri, and the echoings of his horn will arouse the brave spirits of that region as in the early days of the war, when, with his gallant little band, he put his foot on one of the main arteries of the enemy and defied his trained legions.

Since writing the above, we have seen a proof-impression of the engraving accompanying this sketch. The artist has flattered the original by making the features more regular and more youthful-looking than they really are. Lest any of our young lady readers shall fall in love with the General, on seeing his picture, we take occasion to inform them that he is a married man, with two or three children.—*Illustrated News.*

OFFICIAL REPORT OF THE NAVAL ENGAGEMENT AT GALVESTON, TEXAS.

HEADQUARTERS GALVESTON, TEXAS.

This morning, the 1st January, at 3 o'clock, I attacked the enemy's fleet and garrison at this place, and captured the latter and the steamer Harriet Lane, and two barges, and a schooner of the former. The rest, some four or five, escaped ignominiously under cover of a flag of truce. I have about six hundred prisoners and a large quantity of valuable stores, arms, etc. The Harriet Lane is very little injured. She was carried by boarding from two high-pressure cotton steamers, manned by Texas cavalry and artillery. The line troops were gallantly commanded by Colonel Green, of Sibley's brigade, and the ships and artillery by Major Leon Smith, to whose indomitable energy and heroic daring the country is indebted for the successful execution of a plan which I had considered for the destruction of the enemy's fleet. Colonel Bagby, of Sibley's brigade, also commanded the volunteers from his regiment for the naval expedition in which every officer and every man won for himself imperishable renown.

(Signed)   J. BANKHEAD MAGRUDER,
Major General.

INTERESTING ORDER OF MAJOR GENERAL MAGRUDER—COMPLIMENTARY ACKNOWLEDGMENT OF THE DARING AND GALLANTRY OF OFFICERS AND MEN WHO VIED WITH EACH OTHER IN THE GREAT NAVAL ENGAGEMENT WITH THE BLOCKADING FLEET ON THE COAST OF TEXAS.

HEADQUARTERS DISTRICT OF TEXAS,
NEW MEXICO AND ARIZONA,
Houston, Texas, March 11, 1863.

General Orders, No. 45.

The Commanding General, having been prevented by various circumstances from acknowledging the services of the brave Major Watkins, and the gallant officers and men under his command, in the recent victory at Sabine Pass, takes this occasion to return them his official thanks for the accomplishment of a purpose of great importance to us, and their participation in an exploit almost unparalleled in the annals of warfare. After driving the enemy's blockading squadron from our immediate waters, these devoted and heroic men, in their frail boats, pursued him some thirty miles to sea, and after a fight of nearly two hours, on an element on which he considered himself invincible, captured a ship of war of nine guns and an armed schooner of two guns, of the United States Navy, forcing their commanding officers to surrender at discretion. The perseverance, industry and firmness of the commanding officer, Major Oscar M. Watkins, of the Provisional Army, were only equalled by his intrepidity, admirable coolness, and skill in battle. Entirely unaccustomed to the sea, his devotion overcame all obstacles. He was ably and heroically seconded by Captains Fowler and Johnson, respective commanders of the steamers Bell and Uncle Ben, by Captains Odium, O'Brien, Nolen and Aycock, Lieutenants Dowling and Aiken, of the land forces, and by the engineers, pilots, troops and crews of the expedition.

The Commanding General takes pleasure in announcing to the officers and men of Texas, land and naval, that their heroic example has been followed successfully throughout the Confederacy. The echo of their cannon at Galveston and Sabine had not died away ere they were taken up at Charleston, and reverbrated in glory along the Mississippi.

His Excellency, the President, has addressed a letter of congratulation and thanks to the Commanding General and gallant men of Texas, engaged in these noble enterprises. Congress has unanimously passed a vote of thanks, in acknowledgment of their services. The whole country has been electrified by the daring and skill of Texans, while the hearts of their comrades, battling in the North for their homes and altars, have been made to beat with pride and joy, by the news of battles fought and victories won on the beloved soil of their glorious State. To the true soldier there can be no greater reward.

Much has been done; but much remains to be done. Our mortal foe is again gathering his strength for another and still another blow; but the Commanding General of the Army of Texas is confident that his troops will return these blows, and will astonish still more their enemies and the world, by such evidences of skill and audacity, as shall make Texan a better word than Spartan.

With this assurance, he leaves for a short time this immediate scene of his labors, to secure other points and prepare other fields of glory, confident that the officers and men of his command will use all the means in their power to perfect themselves in such a knowledge and practice of their profession as will ensure the fulfilment of the highest expectations of their friends and country.

By command of J. BANKHEAD MAGRUDER,
Major General.
STEPHEN D. YANCEY, A. A. A. G.

YANKEE ACCOUNT OF THE CAPTURE OF THE DIANA.

PORT HUDSON, April 4.

The New Orleans "Era," of the 2d inst., contains the particulars of the capture of the Federal gunboat Diana, on Sunday last, a few miles above Brashear City, on Atshafalaya Bayou, by a portion of Sibley's command. It says: "The Diana was commanded by Captain Peterson, and had aboard Company A, 12th Connecticut, and Company F, 16th New York—in all, one hundred and twenty officers, privates and sailors, all of whom fell into the hands of the Confederates, together with the boat. She mounted one thirty-four pounder Parrott, two thirty-two smooth bores, and two twelve pounder guns. The boat was badly damaged. The report of the engagement at Atchafalaya was distinctly heard at Brashear City. General Weitzel commanding, immediately sent the gunboat Calhoun to assist the Diana, but having no pilot, the Calhoun grounded and came near sharing the same fate. A South wind raised the water and released the Calhoun. The Confederate loss was unknown. The Federals lost three officers and two privates killed."—1863.

MEN WHOSE NAMES SHOULD NEVER DIE.

When Brigadier General Garland, of Virginia, fell mortally wounded on the bloody field of Sharpsburg, his Aid rode up to the dying hero with the inquiry, "Are you hurt, General?"

"Yes," he answered, "I am dying—go tell the senior Colonel of this Brigade to assume command."

Was there ever a more illustrious example of devotion to duty than this? Does history furnish a parallel? The name of

Garland might might well be inscribed on a monument to those whose latest breath murmured forth the accents of patriotism.

But not among Generals alone do we find ever memorable illustrations of all that is ennobling and all that is divine in human impulses and character. The armies of the South furnish from among the common soldiery instances of heroism and of an inextinguishable love of glory which no recorded example of human greatness transcends in ennobling characteristics.

When Sergeant Spithaler, of the Swiss Rifles, fell mortally wounded on the battle-field of Perryville, his thigh crushed and torn by a cannon shot, Colonel Tyler, his commanding officer, went to him, saying, "let me have you removed to the rear."

"No?" said the expiring officer, "let me die on the battle-field."

His name should never be stricken from the roll of his company, and whenever it is called, let some war worn comrade answer as was done for one who fell thus in the old war for independence—let some old veteran answer, "*Dead on the Field.*"

THE CONFEDERATE NAVY.

Since the days of Paul Jones there have been no achievements of a single ship in naval warfare as brilliant as those of the Alabama. Captain Semmes has won for himself and his country imperishable laurels. The Florida, which has just put to sea, under her gallant commander, bids fair to rival the renown of the Alabama. The Navy Department and the Confederate Congress ought to devote their utmost energies to putting more ships afloat, and giving an opportunity to our gallant naval officers to distinguish themselves and render service to the Confederacy. The ocean is the only arena upon which we can carry on aggressive warfare against the Yankees, and touch them in the vital spot of both their pride and interests. The extreme sensitiveness manifested in their commercial circles to the operations of a single ship, the Alabama, shows us their weak spot, and we should strike at it with all our power. With all the boasted prowess of the Yankees upon the deep, we believe that a Confederate navy can be built up which will make the sea as uncomfortable to them as the shore, and drive their commerce—the source of all their wealth—from the face of the ocean.—*Dispatch.*

THE EARLY CAREER OF THE FLORIDA—SEVEN VESSELS DESTROYED.

The privateer Oreto ran the blockade of Mobile, on the 13th January, 1863, notwithstanding there were nine United States vessels of war stationed off the bar, and with full information that she was meditating an escape. The steamers Cuyler and Oneida chased the Oreto, the latter of which had returned to the fleet off Mobile. It is supposed that the Cuyler followed the Oreto to Havana, to which place it was thought that she would go. On her way to Havana she destroyed the brig Ratelle, of Boston.

On the afternoon of the 22d, four miles from the coast, the pirate fell in with the brig Windward, Captain Roberts, from Matanzas, with a cargo of molasses for Portland. The Windward was seized and burned, and the crew sent ashore in their own boat. Her cargo belonged to Spanish merchants. On the morning of the 23d, off Cardenas, the Oreto captured and burned the brig Cora Ann, of Mechias, Maine, Captain Small, from Philadelphia, laden with shucks. She was burnt only one mile from land and the captain and crew sent into Cardenas in their own boat. Soon after, the Oreto captured two more brigs, just out from Cardenas, burned one and sunk the other. A schooner, which arrived at Havana on the morning of the 28th states that the Oreto was last seen with the British flag flying, steering for the Bahamas.

A letter from Havana, dated 24th January, says: "Nothing is talked of here but the atrocities committed by the rebel pirate Maflit. The Florida has captured and destroyed four merchant vessels with valuable cargoes.

The Florida was pursued, after leaving Mobile, by the Federal steamer Cuyler. Captain Maffitt hauled to, and gave her a shot cutting away the foremast. The Cuyler was so disabled that she had to cease pursuit.

The "World" says that the exploits of the Florida caused profound excitement in New York Thursday, and well they might, as she is as swift as the Alabama, stronger, and carries heavier guns. The Florida is commanded by an officer who believes in fighting.

Thus it will be seen that in her first week's cruise she destroyed seven vessels. Hurrah for the Confederate war steamer Florida.
H. W. R. J.

BRILLIANT NAVAL VICTORY—ACCOUNTS FROM EYE WITNESSES.

In the following we give full particulars of the Confederate Naval victory, by which the blockade of the port of Charleston has been effectually raised:

At about 11 o'clock on Friday night, February 27, the Palmetto State, in command of Captain Rutledge, and with the Flag officer, Commodore D. N. Ingraham on board, together with the Chicora, commanded by Captain Jno. R. Tucker, cast off from the wharf, and with their prows turned seaward steamed across the Cooper. The moon was shining brightly, there was not a cloud on the face of the blue sky, and the surface of the water was smooth and glassy as a mill pond. Nature seemed to smile upon the enterprise, and water, sky and wind presented a most delightful manifestation of the divine favor toward our just and noble cause.

The deep silence that brooded over the water was only broken by the gurgle of the screws, as the iron covered vessels moved slowly over the bay. Having reached Fort Sumter, they came to anchor, and there awaited the going down of the moon.

At three o'clock, the report of two guns echoed through the air. That was the signal for their departure, and once more the gunboats are in motion. Silently they move through the darkness, urging their course with all speed, so as to come upon the unsuspecting war vessels before the dawn of day.

The undertaking promised rich rewards, and the nearer the monsters drew to the hostile ships, the more impertinent and resolved became the gallant men who were beneath their iron roofs. Never did the little vessels seem to move so sluggishly, and most closely did the officers and crew scan the clear horizon, fearing that the light would steal over the sea before they reached the blockading fleet.

But deep darkness is still on the deep, and they are near the enemy. Commodore Ingraham descries a black form just ahead, and the sharp bow of the Palmetto State is turned upon the object. Nearer and nearer with all steam on moves the iron vessel. A crash is heard, and the ram of the gunboat penetrates the wooden side of one of Lincoln's blockaders. And while the water was washing into the hole, the guns of the Palmetto State opened upon the hostile vessel.

The officer in command of the Mercedita, seeing it was folly to contend with such an antagonist, immediately struck his flag and surrendered. In a short time the vessel went down. All this time Captain Tucker, of the Chicora, was laying about him vigorously right and left. The shells from his guns set fire to a large ship of war, and she lowered her flag. He sunk, it is believed, another vessel, and the two monsters threw shot and shell at the other vessels that, seeing the fate that had befallen their comrades, turned their bows to the sea and were making their best speed to get beyond the reach of danger. Not one of them showed any disposition to continue the fight; but, careless of the honor of that flag they profess to adore, their cowardly hearts thoroughly possessed by fear, they fled with all the speed their sails and engines enabled them to command. But though they fled so precipitately, we have no doubt that many of the seventeen carried away with them some painful remembrance of that terrible surprise, while it is positively known that several, who succeeded in making good their escape, were severely injured.

When the morning light broke not one of the fleet was in sight. The gunboats cruised many miles seaward from the bar, but the glasses revealed nothing within the range of vision.

The success of that attack is most gratifying, and coming so soon after the brilliant exploit performed by Magruder, at Galveston, it carries unspeakable joy to the hearts of the country.

We cannot speak in too high terms of praise of the judgment, skill and intrepidity that marked the undertaking, and its successful accomplishment. Had it been possible, the entire fleet would have been sunk or disabled.

Commodore Ingraham, Captain Rutledge and Tucker, and the officers under them, as well as their brave crew, deserve our profound and hearty gratitude.

We are indebted to several friends on board the Palmetto State for the following account of her operations. We also give the account of our Special Reporter, who was on board one of the tenders. These accounts contain all the particulars of the expedition and engagement, and show that it has been a brilliant and glorious success on our side, limited only by the cowardly action of the blockaders. They fled, small and large, without even making a show of fight, notwithstanding the presence of two forty-gun frigates, the Susquehannah and Canandaigua. Their loss, however, is known to be severe. Two of their vessels are known to be sunk, while several were fired and went off in a damaged condition.

THE MOVEMENTS OF THE PALMETTO STATE.

At eleven o'clock Friday night the gunboat Palmetto State, Captain Rutledge, bearing the flag of Commodore Duncan, N. Ingraham, left her mooring and proceeded out the harbor towards Fort Sumter. Abreast of Fort Sumter, she passed the three steamers acting as tenders, the Gen. Clinch, Edwin and Chesterfield. At 4:30 A. M. the Palmetto State crossed the bar, and stood out at sea in the direction of the blockading fleet. At 5:20 A. M. we came up to the United States steamer Mercedita, and were hailed by the watch on deck, when the following colloquy took place:

Watch.—What steamer is that? Drop your anchor—back—back—and be careful, or you will run into us.

Captain Rutledge.—This is the Confederate States steamer Palmetto State.

As the answer was given the Palmetto State, with full steam up, ran into the Mercedita, the bow striking her right about midships and making an entrance of about three feet. At the same time our bow gun was fired with a seven inch incendiary shell. We immediately backed out, when the Mercedita hauled down her flag. They were ordered to send a boat to us, and Lieut. T. Abbot, commanding, came off with a boat's crew and surrendered his vessel in the name of Commodore Stellwagon, of the Mercedita, carrying seven guns, and one hundred and fifty-eight men. He stated that his vessel was in a sinking condition, and begged our officers to relieve them. A shot had pierced her boiler, which had burst and scalded a large number of men. Lieut. Abbott begged Commodore Ingraham to take the men with him on board the Palmetto State, as in their haste to come to us they had neglected to put in the plug, and their small boat was only kept afloat by the strenuous efforts of the men bailing the boat. He also stated that the water in the Mercedita had, at the time of his leaving, already risen as high as the engine floor.

Commodore Ingraham regretted that he could not comply with the request as he had no room to accommodate them aboard of his vessels and no small boats or any other means of affording them relief. Lieut. Abbot then pledged his word of honor for the officers and crew of the Mercedita not to serve in any manner against the Confederate States until regularly exchanged, upon which condition he was sent on board his own vessel. The Mercedita was taken completely by surprise. They were roused from their slumbers by the shock, the men not having scarcely time to dress themselves. Lieut. Abbott and the men with him were nearly all destitute of clothing.

The Palmetto State, leaving the Mercedita to her fate, stood out to sea, and engaged several other vessels of the Abolition blockading fleet, occasionally exchanging shots. The latter, however, fled at our approach, firing at long distances, and leaving us far astern. One or two shots were exchanged with the United States frigate Powhatan. The latter, however, followed the example of her companions, and fled. We then stood Northward, towards the Chicora, which at this time was almost surrounded by the enemy's vessels. At 8 A. M. there being no more of the Abolition fleet in sight, we stood back to the entrance of Beach Channel, having signalled the Chicora to return. On passing we were saluted by Forts Moultrie, Sumter and Ripley, and arrived at the wharf in the city a little before six P. M.

THE MOVEMENTS OF THE CHICORA.

The Chicora, Captain John R. Tucker, started from her wharf at half-past eleven Friday night, and crossed the bar at 4:30 A. M. We commenced action at 5:05. The Palmetto State engaged an Abolition vessel on the right, while we engaged the one on the left. As we passed the blockader on the right, the Palmetto State was lying alongside of her. Keeping on our course, we proceeded to within fifty yards of the vessel on the left, and then gave her a shot from our bow gun, the blockader at the time being under full headway. We rounded to and gave her the full benefit of our broadside guns and after gun. She immediately rang her bell for fire and made signals of distress to the rest of the fleet. The last seen of her by signal officer Saunders, she was stern down very low in the water, and disappeared very suddenly. This vessel is supposed to have gone down. Notwithstanding the Chicora immediately steamed towards her, nothing could be discovered of the vessel.

The Chicora proceeding farther out to sea, stood northward and eastward, and met two vessels apparently coming to the relief of the missing steamer. We engaged them. One of them after firing a few guns, withdrew. Standing to the northward, about daybreak we steamed up to a small side-wheel, two-masted steamers, and endeavored to come to close quarters, She kept clear of us, driving away as rapidly as possible, not, however, without receiving our compliments and carrying with her four or five shots. Shortly after the steamship Quaker City, another side-wheel steamer came gallantly bearing down upon the Chicora and commenced firing at long range. Neither would permit our boat to get within a respectable distance. Two of our shots struck the Quaker City and she left apparently perfectly satisfied, in a crippled condition. Another side-wheel, two-masted steamer, with walking beams now steamed toward the Chicora, coming down on our stern. Captain Tucker perceiving it, we rounded to, and proceeded until within about five hundred yards, when the belligerent steamer also rounded to, and gave us both broadsides, and a shot from her pivot gun. We fired our forward gun with an incendiary shell, and struck her just forward of her wheel-house, setting her on fire, disabling and stopping her port wheel. This vessel was fired both fore and aft, and volumes of smoke observed to issue from every aperture. As we neared her she hauled down her flag and made a signal of surrender, but still kept under way with her starboard wheel, and changing her direction. This was just after daybreak. We succeeded in catching this vessel, but having surrendered, and the Captain supposing her boiler struck and the escaping steam preventing the engineers from going into the engine room to stop her; ordered us not to fire. She thus made her escape. After this vessel had got out of our reach, to the perfectly safe distance of about three miles, she fired her last rifled gun, again hoisted her flag, setting all sails, and firing her rifled gun repeatedly at us as she left.

The Chicora now engaged six more of the enemy's vessels at one time—three side-wheel steamers and three propellers—all at long range. Discovering that the flag boat, Palmetto State, standing in towards the shore, orders were given to follow her. On our return we again came across a three-masted bark rigged vessel, which we engaged, firing our guns as we passed, striking her once or twice. We then kept on our course to the Bar, having sustained no damage in the action, nor a single casualty on board. The last ship mentioned above kept firing at us until we got clear out of range, and we giving them our return compliments. One of the blockaders was certainly sunk. We engaged her at the distance of only one hundred yards, and she settled down with her stern clear under water.

The Chicora anchored in Beach Channel, at 8:30 A. M., and arrived at her wharf in the city about six o'clock, receiving a salute from all the forts and batteries as she passed on her return. The number of shots fired by the Chicora during the whole engagement was twenty-seven, mostly incendiary shells. Lieut. Gaskell commanded the forward pivot gun, assisted by Midshipman Pinckey; Lieutenant W. H. Wall, the after pivot; Master Mason, the starboard broadside; Master Payne, the larboard broadside.

The different divisions were commanded by 1st Lieut. G. H. Bier and Lieut. J. C. Claybrook, assisted by Midshipmen R. H. Bacot and Signal Officer Saunders.

The Pilots of the Chicora were Messrs. Thomas Payne and Aldrich.

The results of the engagement are: Two vessels sunk, four set on fire, and the remainder driven away.

CAPTURE OF THE GUNBOAT ISAAC SMITH, IN STONO RIVER.

The Isaac Smith, which was captured in Stono River by our troops, is an iron-screw steamer of 453 tons, and carried eight eight-inch navy guns or sixty-eight pounders and seven-inch thirty pound Parrot gun. She was commanded at the time by Capt. F. S. Conover. Her crew consisted of eleven officers and one hundred and five men, of whom eight were killed and fifteen wounded. She was towed up on Saturday morning by the steamer Sumter to a place of safety under the guns of Fort Pemberton, and will probably be brought to the city to-day for repairs. The Parrot gun was brought on the Sumter, on Sunday morning, to the city, and now lies on Southern wharf.

The steamer's upper works are badly damaged by our shot, and the masts pierced with bullets. Her sides also give evidence of the accuracy of our shot. She will be repaired immediately and made ready for sea. Ninety-three prisoners, including three negroes, arrived in the city on Saturday morning, under escort of a detachment of the Charleston Battalion. They were taken to Gen. Ripley's Headquarters, and ordered to the Provost Marshal's Office, Lieut. Col. Gaillard, who registered their names and turned them over to the care of Mr. Milligan, at the Charleston jail.

From one of the prisoners, who appears to be a very intelligent person, we gather the following account:

"Early Friday morning we were practicing at a target on Cole's Island. In the afternoon started up Stono River and dropped anchor a little above Grimball's plantation. We were preparing supper and the mess were piped up when a battery immediately above us on James' Island, opened fire. The first shot that struck us entered the stern of the vessel, demolishing our crockery, kettles, &c., killing three men, besides wounding others. This shot apparently came from a clump of trees. We immediately got up anchor, and the men beat to quarters. Our guns were fired in the direction of the battery from were the shot came, when another cross firing was opened on the boat from a battery right ahead, supposed to be at Legare's place on John's Island. We ran down as far as the turning of the river, where some wooden spiles were driven in; another battery now opened on us, raking the vessel fore and aft and amidships. The boat had gone a little further when a shot struck the steam condenser, and crippling the machinery, put a stop to our further progress. We then struck our flag and surrendered the boat. After the surrender, the gunboat Commodore McDonough steamed up to the assistance of the Isaac Smith, and commenced firing, as the prisoners were landing, the Smith's Ensign and Pennant at the time having been turned. The Isaac Smith has been in service in Stono River about four months.

———

CHARLESTON, February 1.

The following is the official proclamation in regard to the raising of the blockade:

HEADQUARTERS NAVAL AND LAND FORCES, }
Charleston, S. C., Jan. 31, 1863.   }

About the hour of five o'clock, this morning, the Confederate States Naval Forces on this station attacked the United States blockading fleet off the harbor of the city of Charleston, and sunk, dispersed or drove off and out of sight, for a time, the entire hostile fleet. Therefore, we, the undersigned, Commanders respectively of the Confederate States Naval and Land Forces in this quarter, do hereby formally declare the blockade by the United States of the said city of Charleston, S. C., to be raised by a superior force of the Confederate States, from and after this 31st day of January, A. D., 1863.

(Signed) G. T. BEAUREGARD,
General Commanding.

(Signed) D. N. INGRAMAM,
Commanding Naval Forces in South Carolina,.

Official: THOS. JORDAN, Chief of Staff.

———

RICHMOND, January 31.

The Secretary of State has notified the Foreign Consuls that he has received official information of the opening of the blockade off Charleston.

The belief here is that the blockade cannot be renewed within sixty days.

The Foreign Consuls here (Charleston) held a meeting last night. They are unanimously of the opinion that the blockade of this port is legally raised.

CONFEDERATE VICTORY—YANKEE ARMADA REPULSED WITH GREAT LOSS.

At Charleston, on the evening of the 7th of April, 1868, at half-past two o'clock, the Yankee fleet of Monitors, accompanied by the Ironsides, made an attack upon Fort Sumter with a view to reducing that famous stronghold. They concentrated their fire mainly upon that Fort. A considerable quantity of metal was, however, thrown at Fort Moultrie and Battery Bee. As the fleet approached the winding of the channel brought them within six hundred yards of Fort Moultrie, which gave her an opportunity to fire the first gun in the glorious repulse of that boasted invulnerable Yankee fleet.

The steamer Passaic was the leader in the attack. After an engagement of twenty minutes she retired disabled, and was soon followed by seven others, all in turn having received a severe castigation. The Keokuck remained longest in the conflict, having trusted in her vaunted invulnerability. Scarce twenty minutes sufficed, however, for her to adopt the proverb, "He that fights and runs away, may live to fight another day," and withdrew from the scene of action, in a sinking condition, about five o'clock in the evening. Thus ended in one single day, aye, in a few short hours, the attack upon Charleston; the preparations for which required full two years of time and a cost of upwards of one hundred millions of dollars to the Abolition Yankee nation.

It is an established fact that the troops in the various forts and batteries constituting the bay and harbor defences of Charleston with a universal shout of joy leaped to their guns when they saw the hour of trial of their skill, the strength of their works and the virtue of their guns and mettle was at hand. The first volley from each fort and battery was accompanied with a shout of defiance that rend the air and reverberated from fort to fort and from battery to battery.

They felt every confidence in their ability to frustrate the devices of the foe, and with a determination to do, or die, in the protection of that famed city, from the poluting presence of a hated enemy who with boastful threats and the most formidable preparations had made his appearance.

But, while speaking of the valor and daring of our troops (that manned the guns which have done such terrible execution in) sinking the Keokuk, the most formidable double-turreted

Monitor and disabling eight others who in time withdrew from
the contest to save themselves from destruction, having thought
prudence the better part of valor,) we must not forget the
proper head, the ever-vigilant and sagacious leader General
Beauregard, who some days previous, through mysterious
sources of information, expected an attack at an early day; that
intelligence received confirmation on Sunday morning, when
four Monitors, the Ironsides and thirty vessels of various sizes
were seen off the Bar. Four Monitors and thirty-five wooden
vessels were added to the fleet, the following day thirty-five
vessels, for the most part transports, appeared in the Stono, and
the enemy landed a force of about six thousand men on Coles'
and Battery Islands. These facts, with other indications, lead
General Beauregard to count upon an attack on Tuesday, and
the expectations of that sagacious and watchful General were
realized.

Between two and three o'clock in the afternoon a dispatch
from Col. Rhett, commandant of Fort Sumter, informed Gen.
Beauregard that the fleet were approaching the fort. The
action was opened, by Fort Moultrie firing the first gun. Fort
Sumter opens ten minutes later. Battery Bee, Forts Wagner
and Beauregard, and the Battery at Cummins' Point, also,
opened, firing by battery. The fleet fired with great rapidity;
our forts and batteries replies with spirit and singular accuracy. The Ironsides took position to the left at Fort Sumter,
directing all her guns at that Fort, and throwing shells exclu-
sively.

It was manifest that the Ironsides appointed to test the
strength of the fort, whose reduction was the inauguration of
the terrific contest now going on. Fort Sumter acknowledge
the compliment of the preference by pouring the contents of
her biggest guns into the sides of that pride of the Yankee
navy, and she was not treated with contempt by the other forts
and batteries.

About forty-five minutes after the engagement began, steam
was seen issuing, in dense volumes, from the Ironsides, and she
withdrew from the action, taking position to the south of Fort
Sumter, but remaining a silent spectator of the exciting scene.
She was seriously damaged.

The fight continued till forty-five minutes past five o'clock,
when the last of the fleet, the Keokuk, steamed away and came

to anchor off Morris' Island, where she sunk. Next morning only her smoke stack remained visible.

During the battle, a drummer boy, named Abreene, was killed at Fort Sumter and five men wounded, two severely in the head, the other slightly. A shot passed through Fort Sumter's flag.

Colonel Rhett was in command of Fort Sumter, Col. Butler, of Fort Moultrie, Capt. Sitgraves of Fort Beauregard, Lieut. Col. Simkins of Battery Bee, Major Huger of Battery Wagner, and Lieut. Lesevne, with a detachment from Fort Sumter, of the Battery on Cummins' point.

Fort Sumter was hit thirty-four times, but received no material injury. Six men belonging to Captain Mathews' Artillery Company, stationed at Battery Wagner, were wounded. Two of these have since died. Two were very seriously wounded, and it was thought one would die before morning. The other two, including an officer, were but slightly wounded.

The last gun was fired by the enemy at half-past five, P. M.

There were no casualties at the Cummins' Point Battery.

The flag staff of Fort Moultrie was shot away and one man killed by its fall. The fort itself received no injury whatever. The chimney of one house was taken off by a ball and the roof of another house was struck by a fragment of shell.

Thus is summed up the amount of damage sustained in that terrible and formidable attack by the hated Yankees, who came with a fixed purpose to destroy the cradle of secession and the nest of rebellion, (according to their version.)

The Keokuk was one of the most powerful of her class, and her loss will be a staggering blow to the enemy. She was built last spring and summer, in accordance with plans furnished by Mr. Whitney, an iron merchant of New York, and was said to be impervious to the largest shot or shell capable of being thrown from the most formidable fortification. Her armament consisted of two fifteen inch Dahlgreens—one in each turret. Thus ends one of the boasted invulnerable fleet, which, it has long been trumpeted forth, could not be sunk, but would demolish and wipe out everything that opposed their progress.

The results, so far, has elated our people and given the highest satisfaction to our military commanders.

The nondescript, or "Yankee Devil," for clearing the channel, was washed ashore on Morris' Island yesterday, and is now in our possession. It is described as an old scow-like vessel, painted red, with a long protruding beak and jutting iron prongs or claws, intended for the removal and bursting of torpedoes. It was attached to the Passaic, the leading vessel, and managed by her during the engagement.

Two of the small boats belonging to the Keokuk have been secured by our men on Morris' Island.

It is a curious coincidence of war that the commanders Generals Beauregard, Ripley, Colonel Rhett, Lieut. Col. Yates, and nearly all the garrison of Fort Sumter, were the same men who were the chief actors in the bloodless reduction of Fort Sumter in April, 1861, and who have now so gloriously and successfully repelled a formidable attack upon this famous fortress, while in their keeping.

A YANKEE ESTIMATE OF GEN. BEAUREGARD.

The New York "World," in speaking of the fight at Charleston, makes the following allusion to Gen. Beauregard:

One result of this Charleston fight will be to restore Beauregard to the favor of the Southern people. True, he is boastful, egotistical, untruthful, and wanting in fact, but he is certainly the most marvelous engineer of modern times. By his genius and professional skill he has erected batteries in Charleston harbor that would sink all the wooden fleets of the world did they come under fire, and he has succeeded, moreover, in driving back in disgrace, the most impenetrable iron-clad fleet afloat. There is no denying what this man has done, unpalatable though it may be to the Northern people.

But why should the enemy seem to think that Gen. Beauregard had lost favor among the people in the Confederacy, was it because he so greatly defeated the Yankees at Corinth, by retreating and saving his little army from destruction and utter annihilation, when the enemy had completed their fortifications and entrenchments, having had in position three hundred guns. Or was it because he had broken down his constitution by fifteen months of almost incessant service in the field, having figured most conspicuously in various campaigns that have resulted in crowning him with undying fame, "not only in the Confederacy but in Europe." His tenacity of purpose, his indomitable will and energy united with his invaluable engineering capacity, have caused his name to be heralded among the people and nations of the earth as one of the great Generals of the age. H. W. R. J.

P. S. Probably our Northern enemy, like some of the people

in the Confederacy, knew not what had become of Gen. Beauregard while he was at the springs in Alabama recruiting his health, but since the repulse and terrible disaster to the Federal fleet at Charleston the enemies journalists have again pronounced him as one of the principal actors upon the stage in this terrible drama of revolution and war. H. W. R. J.

THE FIGHT AT CHARLESTON.

For a proper appreciation of our victory at Charleston I give the following extract. Referring to the fight at Charleston the New York "Herald" says:

The guns of the forts were of the heaviest calibre and most approved patterns—the English allies of the rebels having supplied them with some of their best ordnance. The artillery practice was excellent, as is proved by the fact that our nine vessels were struck five hundred and twenty times.

The "Herald" says editorially:

The repulse of Admiral Dupont's iron-clad fleet at Charleston indefinitely postpones, we suspect, the resumption of active operations against the rebel stronghold. The door will, doubtless, be kept more closely guarded than heretofore against English blockade runners, with their "aid and comfort to the enemy;" but, as the sickly summer season in a few weeks will revisit the South Carolina seaboard, we conclude that nothing but some overwhelming Union successes in other quarters will secure the capture of Charleston before the return of the malaria killing frosts of autumn. Indeed, it is broadly hinted in a leading abolition journal that the idea of a crushing spring campaign has been abandoned at Washington, and that probably our military operations, until the end of the summer, will be limited to pegging a little here and there, as the occasion may invite or demand.

The failure at Charleston, together with the failure at Vicksburg, to gain any decisive advantage over the enemy, has, at all events, put an end to the late confident expectations of the country in regard to a vigorous and decisive prosecution of the war.

The "Herald" gives the following as the situation:

The attempt to take Charleston is for the time abandoned. The iron-clad fleet of Admiral Dupont and the army of General Hunter have been withdrawn to Port Royal. The experiment proved too hazardous. The batteries of the enemy at Sumter, Moultrie and Cummings' Point, and the obstructions in the channels, presented obstacles too formidable to be overcome by the force brought against them. By the arrival of the Arago from Charleston Bar on the 11th instant, we learn these facts. The fire from the batteries was tremendous, as the condition of the Keokuk shows. She was fairly riddled through and through with highly polished steel shot, weighing a hundred pounds each, furnished to the rebels by England. Our vessels fired in all one hundred and fifty-one shots at the forts, while the latter struck the boats over five hundred and twenty times.

WAILING AND GNASHING OF TEETH BY THE YANKEES—THE LAST HOURS OF THE KEOKUK.

A New York paper of the 15th instant has the following in reference to the sinking of the Keokuk:

OFF CHARLESTON BAR, April 8.

In coming out of the action yesterday, the Keokuk had the advance, and before she had arrived at the buoy I was alongside of her in a small boat. It was nearly dark at the time; but I could see in the dim light that she had been the target of the most powerful guns the rebels could command. Great holes were visible in her sides, her prow, her after turret and her smoke stack. Her plates were bent and bolts protruded here and there all over her. She was making water rapidly and it was plain to be seen that she was used up and disabled. Before the action her sloping sides and her turrets had been "slushed" with tallow, and to avoid contact with this substance I placed my feet in the shot holes, and literally ascended to her deck as by a ladder. Until that moment I confess my conception of the terrible earnestness with which the rebels had fought was far behind the reality. So thickly did she wear her scars that no one had been able at that time to count them. One round shot penetrated her after-turret, the sides of which, it will be remembered, are frustrums of cones, while the turrets of the Monitors are perpendicular cylinders. Another shot passed through her port bow, and still another through her starboard quarter. These were all steel projectiles of one hundred pounds weight and polished to the smoothness of a knife-blade. The terrible effect of these projectiles may be imagined when it is stated that one of them, striking the after-turret at an angle, when the vessel was almost under the walls of the fort, buried itself in the iron mail, and there remains. These shots, let it be remembered, were furnished to the rebels by neutral Englishmen, and have certainly proved a striking illustration of the fairness and uprightness which characterize the conduct of John Bull toward us in this war.

A WAIL FROM THE TRIBUNE.

A Hilton Head correspondent of the New York York "Tribune" writes: The attack upon Charleston has been made. Our force of offence, collected during the last three months, in the waters and upon the sea islands of South Carolina, have been fairly tried and found wanting. Instead of the pleasant duty of chronicling a triumph to the Union arms, which I had fervently wished rather than hoped, the thankless harbinger of ill-tidings devolves upon me. We have experienced a bitter repulse. The iron-clads have disappointed the expectations of the most confident, and we are mourning over the apparent certainty of an abandonment of the enterprise of which the country, with more faith than reason, hoped such good results.

CHARLESTON IMPREGNABLE.

The New York "Times" thinks Charleston impregnable. In speaking of the fight there it says:

On these natural advantages have been brought to bear the finest engineering skill in the Confederacy (and it was the flower of the genius of the country) during a period of two years. Lee, Beauregard and Ripley in succession have exhausted their professional efforts to make it impregnable. Everything that the most improved modern artillery and unlimited resources of labor can do has been done to make the passage of a fleet impossible. And it is impregnable. Sebastopol was as nothing to it.

Our fleet got but to the entrance of the harbor. It never got within it. Had the iron-clads succeeded in passing the obstructions they would still have found those miles of batteries to run. They would have entered an Inferno which, like the portals of Dante's hell, might well bear the flaming legend, "Who enters here leaves hope behind." Not a point at which they would not have found themselves

"Mid upper, nether, and surrounding fires."

They pass out of the focus of fire of Forts Sumter and Moultrie, Beauregard and Bee, and they find themselves arrested under the ranges of Sumter, the Redan, Johnston and Ripley. Pinckney, the Wappoo battery, and the guns of the city fall upon them! Merely to run by batteries, as was done at the forts below New Orleans, is not a very difficult thing even for vessels not iron-clad; but to be anchored as it were under such fires as these, is what no ships were ever called upon to suffer.

INTERESTING HISTORY OF THE OPENING OF THE ALABAMA'S CAREER.

The London papers all publish the following statement from the late boatswain of the steamer Alabama, now second officer of the British steamer Thistle:

On leaving England, the 290 had a crew of ninety-three men, for the most part belonging to the English Naval Reserve, all being trained gunners, and the majority old men-of-war's men. She was temporarily commanded by Capt. Bullock, who had under him the proper completement of commissioned and petty officers. Captain Bullock having learned that a Federal man-of-war (the Tuscarora) lay in wait for him in St. George's Channel, took his departure by what is known as the North Channel, thus eluding the Federal enemy; though, even had she been intercepted, the Northerner would have found himself in a dilemma, as the 290 had a set of English papers and other presumptive proofs of her neutrality, in the face of which it might have been difficult for her captor to have acted. The 290 at the time carried no guns or other warlike stores, but consisted of the hull, spars and engines, excepting, of course, coal and other requisites to enable her to reach her destination, which was Tarissa, one of the Azores or Western Islands, belonging to Portugal. This destination the 290 duly reached, after a fine run of eight days, and came to anchor in Tarissa Roads, nothing of any moment having occurred to break the usual monotony of a long sea voyage.

Some time before the departure of the 290 from the Mersey, a large bark left the Thames (cleared for Demerara, West Indies,) to meet the 290 at Tarissa, and there transfer to the latter vessel the guns and other stores destined for her, and which formed the cargo of the bark. Some reason required to be assigned to the Portuguese authorities for the 290 having anchored in the bay, and accordingly the excuse furnished by them was that her engines had broken down. This plea was accepted as a valid one, and during the week that intervened between the arrival at Tarissa of the 290 and the bark, the crew of the former vessel were ostensibly engaged in repairing her engines, but really in preparing her to receive her guns, stores, &c.

During this interval, large parties of the inhabitants of Tarissa made daily visits to the 290, their curiosity evidently excited by the war-like appearance of what laid claim to be an English merchant vessel. Many pertinent questions were asked by the Portuguese, and were as ingeniously evaded or met by the officers of the 290. Among other things, the Portuguese wanted to know why the vessel had so many ports, and were told that, as she was bound to a warm climate, they were necessary for ventillation; and when they asked why there was such a numerous crew, reply was, that as she was going on a surveying expedition she required to be well manned. Many similar questions were put, and in like manner answered; but it was all in vain to a'tempt to undeceive the Portuguese, and they would persist in calling her a "frigata Inglesi."

About the lapse of a week from the arrival of the 290 the bark above mentioned sailed in and anchored, her Captain alleging as a reason to the Portuguese officials that his vessel had sprung aleak, which would require to be repaired ere she could resume her voyage; and on this understanding the Portuguese at once placed her in quarantine, (which in the Azores lasts three days.) On the day after the bark's arrival Capt. Bullock, of the 290, being anxious to get his guns on board, hauled alongside the bark, and erected a pair of large shears to effect the transfer of her cargo from the bark's hold to the 290's deck. This brought off the Portuguese in a fury that their rules should have been broken by the 290 having dared to communicate with a vessel that had still two days quarantine to run, and they angrily demanded to know the reason why their regulations had been infringed. They were told that the bark was in a sinking condition, and the erection of the shears was accounted for by urging the necessity of an immediate temporary transfer of her cargo, that the leak might be reached and stopped, and Captain Bullock finally succeeded in bearing down all opposition by feigning to get in a passion, saying he was doing no more for the bark than any Englishman would do for a countryman in distress. The Portuguese left the vessel, and the transhipment proceeded without further hindrance from those on shore.

About the afternoon of the second day, and when the transfer was nearly complete, the British screw steamer Bahama came in, having on board Captain Semmes and the other late officers of the Sumter, besides the remainder of the 290's armament and an addition of twenty odd men to her crew. On the Bahama's arrival and anchorage on a somewhat similar pretext to those given to her two predecessors, the Portuguese fairly lost all patience, and peremptorily insisted on the instant departure of all three vessels. The Bahama at once communicated with the 290, and having hauled over everything destined for her, got up steam and left, followed by the 290, towing the now empty bark. All three went, not to sea, as they had been ordered to do, but to Angra Bay, (a bay in the same island, and only a few leagues distant from Tarissa Roads.) Here they remained unmolested until noon the following day, (a Sunday,) when, for the second time, all three vessels were ordered out of Portuguese waters. All the 290's guns being now mounted, and the vessel otherwise ready for a cruise, the order was obeyed, and all took their departure—the bark, as before, in tow of the 290, which having conveyed her well out to sea, cast her off, and, with a favorite breeze, she steered for Cardiff, to bring out a further supply of coal for the 290's use.

The 290 and the Bahama now steamed round the island, and Captain Semmes, coming out of his cabin, ordered the First Lieutenant to muster the crew aft. This having been done, and all the officers assembled on the poop in their full uniform—i. e., Confederate grey frock coat and trowsers—Captain Semmes enjoined silence, and read his commission as Post Captain in the Confederate navy. It was a document fully attested at Richmond, and bore the signature of "Jefferson Davis, President Confederate States of America." He then opened and read his sealed orders from the President, directing him to assume command of the Confederate sloop-of-war Alabama, hitherto known as the 290, in which, having been duly commissioned, he was to hoist the Confederate ensign and pennant and "sink, burn and destroy everything which flew the ensign of the so-called United States of America." Captain Semmes then ordered the First Lieutenant to fire a gun and run up the Confederate flag and pennant.

The gun was fired by the Second Lieutenant, (Armstrong, a relation of the famous inventor,) and ere its smoke had cleared away, the Stars and Bars of the young Confederacy were floating on the breeze, and the ceremony was complete, Captain Semmes declaring the vessel, henceforth to be known as the Alabama, to have been duly commissioned. The next step was formally to engage the crew to serve and fight under the Confederate flag, which having been done, the men were addressed by their Captain in an eloquent and stirring speech, in the course of which he said there were only four vessels in the United States Navy that were more than a match for the Alabama; but he said that in an English built heart of oak, as she was, and surrounded, as he then saw himself, by British hearts of oak, he wouldn't strike his newly hoisted flag for any one of the four.

Of course this elicited a hearty burst of cheering for President, State and Captain, and when it had subsided, Captain Semmes said the Bahama was on the point of leaving for England, and intimated that if any of his crew repented of the step they had taken, they were free to return in her. This alternative none would accept, and Captain Bullock and a few of the other officers who had taken the 290 from England to the Azores, find their occupation gone through the arrival of those who had held similar appointments in the Sumter, having gone on board the Bahama, the vessel and the Alabama, amidst hearty cheering from the crews of both, parted company, the former pursuing her course back to England, the latter in chase of a Yankee whaler, which she captured and burned. This was her first prize, and her subsequent career is now so famous as to render a single remark thereon superfluous.

The Alabama's crew receive from the Confederate Government half the value of each Federal ship and cargo they destroy, and each of her crew is now worth several hundred pounds. All obligations have hitherto been faithfully discharged in gold. The Alabama is supplied with coal from Wales, by three sailing vessels thus constantly employed.

The Boatswain of the 290, to whom I referred above, having been superseded by the late Boatswain of the Sumter, returned to England in the Bahama.

CONFEDERATE STEAMER ALABAMA—THE LONDON "TIMES" ON THE "290."

The London "Times," in an editorial upon the New York Chamber of Commerce and the Confederate steamer Alabama, takes the ground that no blame can attach to the British Government because such vessels are built and fitted out in England. We copy a portion of the article:

In the old days of Gretna Green marriages, when an enraged guardian drove up to Newman's stables at Bernet just in time to see the fugitive ward driven off by four speedy grays, he turned furiously upon the horsekeeper for having supplied the runaways with such splendid horse flesh. "I am strictly neutral, sir," said the master of the road. "Four bays, the exact counterparts in blood and bone, are harnessing for you at this moment." We cannot shut up our shipping yards, but all the world is free to buy in them. We do not fit out ships of-war, but sell all the competent materials to any one who will buy. It is for them, at their own risk, to take them away and put them together. In doing this we follow very high example, and are covered by very high authority. In 1855, when we were at war with Russia, some of us had some foolish notion that we ought to have the sympathy of a kindred race and a free Government. We were inclined to expostulate when we found America selling to our enemy the chief materials by which he carried on the war. But what did Mr. President Pierce answer? He showed us at once how wrong we were. He professed the purest neutral policy. * * * *

We have never gone beyond, or even stepped fully up to the bounds of American theory. That theory, however, is perfectly sound, and therefore it is that we sell unarmed ships to the world, "regardless," as Mr. President Pierce so aptly says, "of the destination of these articles." The New York Chamber of Commerce had better send Capt. Wilkes to the Alabama. We cannot undertake to capture this one Confederate cruiser. We are very sorry that the Brilliant was burnt, and so we are that the towns on the Mississippi were burnt, and that murder and dishonor of men and women of Alabama took place. These scenes are said to have suggested the name of this terrible cruiser; but we know our duties as neutrals, and we sit as disciples at the feet of President Pierce.

CONFEDERATE STEAMER ALABAMA.

The following will give some idea of the rapidity of movement of the Alabama, and her efficiency in operating upon Yankee commerce. H. W. R. J.

The Confederate war steamer Alabama is still operating successfully on the commerce of the United States. A ship has arrived at New York from Port Petrie, brought the crew of the ship Levi Starbuck, which was captured and burned by the Alabama on the 2d of November, when five days out. On the 8th of November, the Alabama captured and burned the ship T. B. Watts, of and for Boston, from Calcutta, with a valuable cargo of saltpetre, gunny cloth, &c. The Alabama put into Port Petrie on the 17th, and landed the Captains and crews of the three ships. The same afternoon the United States steamer San Jacinto arrived outside to wait for the Alabama—but the latter vessel escaped during the night. Captain Semmes boasts that he has been within seventy miles of New York.

THE SEA FIGHT BETWEEN THE HATTERAS AND THE ALABAMA.

The Kingston (Jamaica) Standard, of January 25th, after announcing the arrival of the Confederate States war steamer Alabama, at that port, says:

The Alabama is consigned to Messrs. Charles Levy & Co., of this city, and is now receiving coals, &c., at Port Royal, from Messrs. T. D. Pass & Co. She called into this port to receive casual repairs. Captain Semmes, we learn, waited on his Excellency, the Lieutenant Governor, in Spanish Town, yesterday. Several of the Confederate officers were ashore in grey uniforms, and we learn that the prisoners will be left in charge of the American Vice Consul here. We understand that in the encounter the Alabama received some damage and that several shipwrights and caulkers have been dispatched to Port Royal to repair the damages.

We gather the following additional particulars:

On Sunday, the 11th instant, about 2½ o'clock, the Brooklyn, sloop-of-war, twenty-one guns, Commodore Belt, lying at Galveston, Texas, discovered a sail, which she supposed to be a merchantman running the blockade, and immediately signalized the Hatteras to give chase. The Hatteras pursued her until dark. The Alabama then hove to and awaited her approach. The Hatteras was prepared, and all the men went to quarters. She bespoke the stranger, who replied she was "Her Britanic Majesty's steamer Petrel." Captain Blake, of the Hatteras responded. In the meantime, the Alabama attempted to manœuvre to the stern of the Hatteras. While off the port quarter Capt. Blake said he would send his boat on board; and while in the act of lowering the boat the Alabama sent a blank cartridge astern of the Hatteras. She hailed her and said she need send no boat, as she was the Confederate steamer Alabama. Captain Blake then gave the order to fire and the engagement ensued. In about ten minutes a hole was discovered between wind and water, in the Hatteras. Fire also broke out in the fore peak in the lower deck but was put out. A shot was sent through her steam chest. She then surrendered, being completely disabled. The Alabama sent all her boats to take the crew off, and in a few minutes after this she sunk. Only the ship papers were saved.'

The Alabama made Port Royal in eleven days.

A boat's crew from the Hatteras, seven in number, is missing, supposed to have gone back to Galveston. Little personal injury was sustained on either side.

THE STEAMER ALABAMA AT KINGSTON—A CURIOUS INCIDENT OF THE WAR.

The very curious and exciting incident of a cowhiding between two Kingston merchants had grown out of Captain Semmes' visit. It appears that Capt. Semmes offered for sale here the United States Treasury notes captured from the steamer Ariel, and two merchants of Kingston, in overbidding each other for the booty, got into a quarrel, resulting in the cowhiding of one of the parties by the other.

AN INCIDENT CONNECTED WITH THE SAILING AND RUNNING OF THE BLOCKADE BY THE CONFEDERATE WAR STEAMER FLORIDA.

A correspondent of the Charleston Mercury, writing from Mobile under date of the 19th January, gives the following interesting news in relation to the sailing of the steamer Florida:

A premature statement appeared in a Richmond paper several weeks ago announcing the escape from this port of the Confederate States steam corvette Florida, Capt. Maffit commanding. It was not true, for at that time no effort had been made to escape. Capt. Maffit lingered here so long after his vessel was ready for sea as to call upon himself much criticism and censure and applications from some quarters went on to the Secretary of the Navy requesting his removal from the command of his vessel.

The Secretary at once issued the order relieving him from command. President Davis was then absent from Richmond, and the Secretary acted on his own counsel in the matter; but, happily for Maffit, President Davis arrived in Mobile almost simultaneously with the order of the Secretary. The facts of the delay were explained to the President, who at once restored Maffit to his vessel.

There may be truth in the matter, and even if true, there is much reason why a man who was going abroad for a three years' cruise upon the world of waters, and in far distant seas should linger long and fondly among the fair. Now he is gone the blockaders are dodged, and "the rover is free." I saw him one night when he was bidding adieu to his friends. He said that the weather indicated a strong "northeaster," for which he had been waiting so long, and that he would be off in a few hours. But the indication was not fulfilled. The weather changed, and he remained until last Thursday, the 14th instant, when he escaped just before day.

He attempted it on the night previous, but the blo kaders discovered him and signaled, when he withdrew. Thursday night was very dark. There was a strong blow and a hailstorm during several hours. He ran out unobserved. But about four hours after his escape, they either discovered or suspected that he was gone, and the swiftest steamer among them went to sea, apparently in pursuit. She will hardly catch him.

The Florida is a splendid vessel, in perfect running and fighting trim, and can, probably, whip any craft that she cannot outrun. Maffit is as brave as Nelson, as shrewd as a fox, and as thorough a seaman as ever trod a deck. His escape cannot long remain a secret, even if it be one now, for Yankee journals will soon teem with details of his operations. Those who know him well predict for him a career as glorious as that of Semmes.—1863.

THE TERRORS OF THE SEA—CAREER OF THE FLORIDA—DESCRIPTION OF HER OFFICERS AND STYLE.

The Yankee papers have a new sensation in the Florida and two Confederate sailing privateers, which are just out—the Retribution and Dixie. These sailing vessels are schooners of about 160 tons, both painted black. The captain and crew of the brig Estelle, which was destroyed by the Florida, have arrived in New York. The Estelle was bound for Boston, with sugar and honey, and first descried the Florida on the 19th ult., off Cape Antonio. The following is a description by her first mate of the Florida's style of taking prizes:

The brig was all the time under close reefed sails. Captain Brown, her commander, at first thought the stranger might be the Alabama; but, as she had the stars and stripes flying, this opinion gave way to the belief of her being a Federal cruiser.

Shortly before 3 o'clock, P. M., the steamer, which had come up abreast of the brig to a distance of seventy-five yards, fired a shot across her bows, and lowering the American flag ran up that of the Confederacy. Her guns were brought to bear on the Estelle, whose captain thus was made aware of his fate. The Estelle at once backed her topsail and hove to, when five boats were lowered from the Confederate steamer and pulled towards the doomed brig. The second lieutenant of the Florida stepped on board, and respectfully saluting the captain, remarked, "Captain, you are a prize to the Southern Confederacy. Pack up your private property with all dispatch and let your crew do the same." This order was at once complied with, when the crew were ordered on board the steamer.

The lieutenant sent the chronometer, charts and instruments of the brig on board the steamer, and selected from the ship chandlery stores and cargo such articles as were wanted on the steamer. He then set his crew to work in stripping the brig of a part of her rigging, all her sails, except foretop gallantsail, royal and main staysail and foretop staysail, which were sent on board. A fire was then kindled on the deck, both fore and aft, and in a few minutes the brig was a mass of flame.

When the crew of the brig arrived on the steamer, they were at once informed by the first lieutenant that they would be treated as prisoners of war, and allowed the liberty of the ship, provided they would conform to the rules of the vessel. They were divided among the crew of the steamer as messmates, and had the same fare as their captors. The captain of the brig was at once invited to partake of the hospitalities of the cabin, and a state-room was at once arranged for himself and mate. The second mate was sent to mess with the subaltern officers. The fare of the officers and crew of the Florida was nearly the same—salt beef, peas and rice, with an allowance of hard bread. The officers, however, said that in Havana they would be fully supplied with all necessaries for a long cruise.

The officers of the Florida treated their prisoners with great delicacy and kindness and, during frequent conversations on the _____ ___ ____ed, with tears in their eyes, that the stern necessities of war obliged them to fight their brethren of the North. They are mostly ex-officers of the navy, and exact the same discipline of their crew as on the United States men-of-war. No profane or insulting language is allowed, and the offender punished severely.

The first lieutenant is Mr. Heid, who had just returned from the Pacific, when he tendered his resignation to the United States authorities. The Chief Engineer, Spydee, is a native of middle Tennessee, where he lost all of his property. He is said to be very proficient in his business.

The officers of the Florida state that they ran out of Mobile on a clear, starlight night, with a fresh breeze, and that they ran past seven Federal gunboats, none of which fired a single shot at them.

They were chased until next morning by two gunboats, but then they left their pursuers far astern and hull down. Captain Maffit stopped the steamer until the Federals were in full sight, when he crowded on steam until he lost sight of them. The Florida's officers stated that there were five more steamers in Mobile ready to run the blockade, and for aught they knew were already at sea.

The crew is a mixture of all nationalities, but the English and Irish element predominates. There are some Eastern men among them, and one of them named Layton, a native of Portland, Maine, is the boatswain. There is also one Chinaman on board. Most of the crew have been prisoners of war at the North, and some of them were in Fort Columbus, or in the Pea Patch, near Philadelphia.

They are well drilled in the use of the guns, and are far superior to many of our merchant crews.

THE CONFEDERATE WAR STEAMER FLORIDA AT BARBADOES.

The New York "Herald" of a recent date contains the following:

BARBADOES, February 25.

Great is the excitement in this fast anchored isle of Barbadoes. The rebel steamer Florida, Capt. J. N. Maffit, arrived here in distress, asking for coal. It appears that the pirate craft has either had a hard mauling or a rough handling by the "ocean monarch."

The Florida seems to be well disciplined, the men well behaved and orderly, the officers polite and attentive.

The Florida privately takes a mail for France and England. She went out in splendid style.

From the station lookout the Florida was seen at 5, P. M., to fire three vessels, some ten miles from the Barbadoes shore.

A large side wheel steamer, presumed to be the Vanderbilt, went after the rebel, who seemed hove to, ready for a muss. We are all excitement and anxiety here. No cannonading has been reported, only the echo of one or two heavy guns.

Everybody who can get an elevated position is looking out for the "sea fight." One of the vessels burned was a splendid guano ship, with guano on board. The crew are landing.

The Florida is now seen, all right, steering north by east. She is bound for the English Channel. This is sure.—*April*, 1863.

THE RETRIBUTION.

We had the pleasure yesterday of seeing Capt. Vernon Lock, of the well known privateer Retribution, which has been a terror to Yankee commerce in the Gulf, only second to the Alabama and Florida.

It is no secret that the Retribution is the old tug Uncle Ben, fitted up as a schooner. That a vessel of her class has been able to make herself such a terror to the enemy, speaks volumes for the boldness and enterprise of her officers and crew.

Charleston Courier, April, 1863.

A COMPLIMENT TO LIVERPOOL.

The Northern papers and their European correspondents, referring to the naval preparations of the "Rebels," remarks:

But it is the Liverpool Southern Association that the rebels most largely owe whatever of credit and resources they possess in England. Liverpool is bitterly and almost unanimously rebel in its sympathies, and throughout Great Britain this pestilent seaport has exerted a wise and earnest influence against us. We are not likely to forget it.

A fact concerning the Alabama deserves to be stated. The American Consul at Liverpool seems to have made every effort to persuade the British authorities to prevent her from leaving port on a cruise which all men knew was to be piratical. The Government at last consented to interfere, and the day after the Alabama had sailed, issued an order restraining her from going to sea.

It is evident, from such facts as the above, which are important, and comes to us well authenticated, that the rebels have no lack of money or credit in England. Probably a considerable part of the cotton hypothecated to the rebel government, is pledged in some way to English capitalists as security for advances, and they in turn are secured by insurances at an extravagant premium, but with margin enough to make themselves good.

A RATTLESNAKE ON THE OCEAN.

On Tuesday night, the privateer Rattlesnake ran the gauntlet of the blockading fleet at the mouth of the Ogeechee River and steamed away on the broad ocean on her mission of destruction of Yankee commerce. She is not a Government war vessel, as was stated by one of our city cotemporaries some time since, but a privateer—about one-fifth of her stock being owned in this city. The Rattlesnake (late Nashville) is commanded by Capt. T. H. Baker, an experienced and competent officer, and more especially qualified for his present business by the brutal and inhuman treatment he has received at the hands of the Yankees. It will be remembered that he was the Captain of the ill-fated Savannah, who, with the rest of her crew, were so long confined in chains in a Northern dungeon. We learn that he has with him the handcuffs he wore while under the protection of the American Eagle, and that he declares his purpose to try them on several pairs of Yankee wrists. No wonder that his soul is all aglow with the passion of revenge. The Rattlesnake is armed to the teeth and will weed a wide row on the ocean. Success to her.—*Columbus Times, February 20, 1863.*

PROGRESS OF THE WAR—AFFECTING INCIDENT--ONE OF THE RESULTS OF THE WAR.

One of the most affecting incidents of the brilliant and successful recapture of Galveston by the forces under Major General Magruder was the meeting (already briefly alluded to between Major Lea, of our army, with his eldest and fondly loved son, who was 1st Lieutenant of the Harriet Lane. The Houston "Telegraph" says:

Nearly two years ago the father, then residing in Texas, had written repeatedly to the son, then on the coast of China, suggesting the principles that should determine his course in the then approaching struggle between the North and the South of the United States and saying that he could not dictate to one so long obligated to act on his own judgment; and that decide as he might, such was his confidence in his high consciousness he would continue to regard him with the respect of a gentleman and the affection of a father; but that, if he should elect the side of the enemy, they would probably never meet on earth, unless perchance they should meet in battle.

The father has served nearly eighteen months eastward of the Mississippi, and, through unsolicited orders, arrived at Houston, en route for San Antonio, late at night of the 30th ult., when, hearing of the intended attack on the Harriet Lane, aboard of which he had heard was his son, also placed there simply in the order of Providence, he solicited permission to join the expedition, in expectation of nursing or burying his son, whose courage was obliged to expose him fatally to the equal daring of our Texas boys. During the fight Major Lea was ordered by the General to keep a look out from a house top for all movements in the bay. As soon as daylight enabled him to see that the Lane had been captured, by permission of the General, who knew nothing of the expected meeting, he hastened aboard, when he was not surprised to find his son mortally wounded. Wading through blood, amidst the dying and the dead, he reached the youth, pale and exhausted. "Edward, 'tis your father." "I know you, father, but cannot move," he said faintly. "Are you mortally wounded?" "Badly, but hope not fatally." "Do you suffer pain?" "Cannot speak," he whispered. A stimulant was given him. "How came you here, father?" When answered, a gleam of surprise and gratification passed over his fine face. He then expended nearly his last words in making arrangements for his wounded comrades. His father knelt and blessed him, and hastened ashore for a litter, and returned just after life had fled.

When told by the surgeon that he had but a few minutes to live, and asked to express his wishes, he answered, confidingly, "My father is here," and spoke not again. He was borne in procession to the grave from the headquarters of Gen. Magruder, in company with his Captain, and they were buried together, with app----iate military honors, in the presence of many officers of ..a armies and many generous citizens, all of whom expressed their deep sympathy with the bereaved father, who said the solemn service for the Episcopal Church for the burial of the dead, and then added this brief address:

"My friends, the wise man has said that there is a time to rejoice and a time to mourn. Surely this is a time when we may weep with those that weep. Allow one so sorely tried, in this his willing sacrifice, to beseech you to believe, whilst we defend our rights with strong arms and honest hearts, that those we meet in battle may also have hearts brave and honest as our own. We have here buried two brave and honest gentlemen. Peace to their ashes! Tread lightly o'er their graves. Amen!
January, 1863.

INCIDENTS OF THE CAPTURE OF THE HARRIET LANE.

Captain William M. Armstrong went on board the Harriet Lane after the battle, and found, lying in the blood, on deck, a Bible. He picked it up and remarked, "Now I am going to open this Bible this new year's day, and the first passage I read I will take as an omen for the new year." He opened it carelessly and the first passage his eye fell on was the first verse of the 20th chapter of Deuteronomy, "When thou goest out to battle against thine enemies, and seest horses and chariots, and a people more than thou, be not afraid of them; for the Lord thy God is with thee!" It is a good omen as well as a most startling circumstance.

One of the Texans who boarded the Harriet Lane immediately jumped aboard, grasped a Federal by the collar, exclaiming, "Surrender, or I will blow your brains out!" The other replied: "You'd better look at me first!" Recognition was instantaneous; they were brothers!

QUEEN OF THE WEST—FURTHER PARTICULARS.

The Jackson (Miss.) "Appeal" of the 21st has the following:
From a gentleman direct from Natchez we have some further particulars of the capture of the Queen of the West.

On Wednesday of last week the Queen ran past Natchez and anchored two miles below. The DeSoto followed her, stopping just above the landing, where she destroyed several flat boats and skiffs. From one of the flats she took three boys prisoners who were raised in Natchez. The Queen of the West remained at anchor in protecting distance, while these depredations were carried out by the DeSoto. They both then steamed away together, the boys having been placed on the Queen of the West.

The two vessels proceeded down the river, entered Red River, and at or near the mouth of the Atchafaylaya Bayou, the Era, No. 5, with a load of corn for Port Hudson, was captured. They were fired upon at the mouth of the Atchafalaya, by a light battery, when the Captain of the Queen was killed. In revenge, they steamed down the bayou and utterly destroyed six plantations by shelling them.

They pressed the pilot of the Era, No. 5, who deceived them as to the location and strength of our batteries. One of the boys captured at Natchez heard Colonel Ellett repeatedly assert that before he would surrender he would blow the boat up, but when he was fired upon by our batteries, his feather immediately wilted and his only anxiety was the safety of his precious person. He was afterwards seen floating down the river on a bale of cotton. The courier has the following report of the affair:

The engagement lasted about one hour, when twenty-five of the crew were taken prisoners, ten or twelve drowned, and Col. Ellett, who was in command of the Queen, cowardly forsook his boat and floated down the stream on a cotton bale. His own crew shot at him for his cowardice.

The Queen had on board six heavy guns. The DeSoto was scuttled and sunk by her crew, as well as the coal boat in tow.

The Era, No. 5, being in possession of the Federal guard below the scene of action, she soon put out to the Mississippi River; bringing with her our informant, Thomas O'Brien, who was afloat in the river on a cotton bale, and who brings this intelligence. About ten miles below Natchez, the Era, No. 5, met the Federal gunboat Indianola, carrying four 11-inch guns, and about two hundred men. Here both boats came to anchor, and our informant made his escape.

Young O'Brien, and two others, were kept on board the Queen of the West as prisoners, during the attack of our batteries. He says that every shell from the Confederate batteries carried destruction to the boat and crew. The first shell completely cleared the gun-deck of her men, and the second or third came crashing through her engines, cutting her steam pipe in twain, and completely disabling the gunboat. She would soon be got off for repairs.

On the Era, when taken, were two Confederate officers and twenty-five privates. The privates were paroled.

The victory on Red River was complete. The amount of stores taken is large.

The prisoners taken from the Queen threaten to shoot Colonel Ellett, for his desertion of them and cowardice, whenever they overtake him.

THE CAPTURE OF THE UNITED STATES GUNBOAT INDIANOLA ON THE MISSISSIPPI—ENEMIES ACCOUNT.

WASHINGTON, March 2, 1863.

The gunboat Indianola has been taken by the rebels below Vicksburg. Two or three rebel steamers, prepared in Galveston style, and filled with armed men, fastened upon the Indianola and captured her. She is iron clad. In conjunction with the Queen of the-West, and the vessels originally possessed by the rebels, they now have quite a fleet below Vicksburg, and it will be necessary for Admiral Porter to send down seven gunboats at once and clear out the rebel musquito fleet. Their operations show the energy of despair, and our own should be prompt and powerful to crush out their last hope.

The language of the correspondent of the above item rather betrays a misgiving and a feeling bordering upon the verge of despair, seeing that we are terribly in earnest to establish our independence and free ourselves from tyranny and despotism, and in future avoid corrupt associations. Poluting and debasing intercourse with a hated race.
H. W. R. J.

SHIPS AGAINST FORTS.

A correspondent of the Savannah "Republican" gives an interesting review of the defence of Fort McAllister:

The defence of Fort McAllister is one of historic interest and marks a historic period, because it was a desperate struggle against odds never before encountered. It stands forth in solitary pre-eminence, and can only be compared with future defences of like character. The annals of all the past furnish no parallel to it. In the history of two or three hundred sieges, from the era of Louis XIV, down to our day, no appropriate standard of comparison can be found. That history appertains generally to land attack and defence. This is the old question of ships against fortifications revived under an aspect absolutely novel. Among the more prominent instances of this description are, the attack of Lord Exmouth on Algiers in the last century; that of Lord Nelson on the Crown Batteries of Copenhagen about the beginning of this, and the comparatively recent attack by Admiral Napier on the defences of St. Jean d'Acre on the coast of Syria. There are other cases less signal, as that at New London during the war of 1812, when two 18-pounder guns beat off two British sloops-of-war. Then, the ships had wooden walls, and in general their projectiles were round shot of small dimensions. The gallant defence of Vicksburg has been justly extolled, but while the attack there was by no means so formidable as that of Genesis Point, the defence was made under conditions vastly more favorable.

Fort McAllister, however, is a simple irregular earthwork, or field fortification, but the parapets are unusually thick and strong. It is quite open in the rear, and its batteries are not casemated. The embrasures in which the heaviest guns are placed are protected by traverses from an enfilading fire, but they are necessarily exposed to a direct one. This field work has grown to its existing proportions by such successive adorations as necessity has dictated, receiving its finishing touches from the plastic hands of Captain McGrady. It would be improper to advert here to the additional development which these entrenchments are now receiving. It may suffice to say that on the 3d instant it was far from formidable. The action was chiefly maintained by its 32-pounder rifled gun and the favorite 42-pounder. One of the traverse wheels of this last gun having been broken by a shell, it was replaced under fire. The 8-inch gun, which did the best execution during the engagement next previous, was dismounted before meridian, by a shot which struck one of the diagonal braces. It was mounted again during the night upon a carriage sent down from Savannah. The 10-inch gun, fired at an elevation of 8.30, generally overshot the tower aimed at. It had been but recently placed in battery, and practice with it was limited.

Opposed to the fort were three iron-clad gunboats and three mortar boats, the former launching, with a direct horizontal fire, projectiles more formidable than any yet known; the latter throwing shells with curved fires, from six o'clock, P. M., during all the night, which did not prevent, however, the reparation of all the damage done during the day. In the Engineer's report, the iron-clads—distant from 1,400 to 1,900 yards—are numbered 1, 2 and 3, No. 1 being up stream. The projectiles hurled by No. 1 were hollow shot and shells of fifteen inches diameter, and also solid shot and shells of eleven inches. Those of No. 2 were cylindro-conoidal percussion shells, eight inches diameter at the base and seventeen inches in length, and eleven inch solid shot and shells. No. 3 threw cylindro-concidal shells like the above. This fire was maintained nearly eight hours, with average intervals of ten minutes. The most active fire appears to have been concentrated on the 42-pounder, in the immediate vicinity of which twenty-one projectiles fell. At this and most other points the happy escape of the garrison seems almost providential.

The fire of the fort was concentrated on Monitor No. 1, the men in No. 3, not on duty, quietly looking on from their deck. Lieut. Ellerby, from his position in the marsh on the left bank of the Ogeechee, only 350 yards distant from No. 3, reports that he could hear the words of command—that her ports were always open, that the guns were run regularly in and out of battery, the rammer staff and the hands of the men being visible, and that the guns were therefore loaded at the muzzle.

One shot from the fort struck the tower a few inches from one of the port holes.

The revolutions of the tower of No. 1 were observed to be often temporarily arrested either from design or injury sustained. The last shot from the 42-pounder struck No. 1 low down, near the water line. This was followed by an escape of steam and the sudden appearance and disappearance of three men. After this she blew her whistle, when No. 2, which had already weighed anchor and started down stream, returned and took her place. Meanwhile No. 1 retiring discharged her guns without aim or object.—*March*, 1863.

THE BATTLE OF GENESIS POINT.

Gen. Beauregard has issued the following order, conveying a well merited tribute to the skill and gallantry of the garrison of Fort McAllister:

HEADQUARTERS DEPARTMENT OF S. C., GA. AND FLA., }
Charleston, S. C., February 6, 1863. }

General Orders, No. 23.

The Commanding General announces to the forces, with satisfaction and pride, the results of the recent encounter of our battery at Genesis Point, Georgia, with an iron-clad of the Monitor class—results only alloyed by the life-blood of the gallant commander, the late Major John B. Gallie.

For hours the most formidable vessel of her class hurled missils of the heaviest calibre ever used in modern warfare, at the weak parapet of the battery, which was almost demolished; but standing at their guns as become men fighting for homes, for honor, and for independence, the garrison replied with such effect as to cripple and beat back their adversary, clad though in impenetrable armor, and armed with 15 and 11-inch guns, supported by mortar boats, whose practice was of uncommon precision.

The thanks of the country are due to this intrepid garrison, who have thus shown what brave men may withstand and accomplish, despite apparent odds.

"Fort McAllister" will be inscribed on the flag of all the troops engaged in the defence of the battery.

By command of General Beauregard.
(Signed)   THOMAS JORDAN, Chief of Staff.

INTERESTING SKETCH OF INGRAHAM AND RUTLEDGE.

We take the following extracts from biographical sketches which have appeared in Yankee papers in reference to the fight off Charleston, in which the Mercedita was sunk into Port Royal:

SKETCH OF COMMODORE INGRAHAM.

Commodore Duncan N. Ingraham, who is over sixty years of age, is the son of the late Nathaniel Ingraham, Esq., of Charleston, S. C., and belongs to a family eminently naval in its character. All of them, with one exception, were officers in the navy. His father being the intimate friend of Captain Paul Jones, volunteered under his command, when he left France in the Bon Homme Richard, in 1779, and fought with him in the battle with the British frigate Serapis, one of the most desperate battles in the annals of naval warfare. His uncle, Capt. Joseph Ingraham, United States Navy, was lost in the United States ship Pickering, which went down at sea, and was never heard of, at the beginning of this century. His cousin, William Ingraham, was killed at the age of twenty when a Lieutenant in the United States Navy.

The sole exception in the family was his uncle, Duncan Ingraham, Esq., from whom he received his name. He was one of the most accomplished gentlemen of his day, and though intimate with the leading political men of our country, yet from taste and early associations he was a loyalist in his views. At the opening of the Revolution in 1774, he went to Europe, and remained there until its close. John Adams, when Commissioner to France in 1779, frequently speaks of him in his diary as his associate in Paris. He returned, however, to this country in 1784, gave in his adherence to the Government, and permitted his son to enter the navy—the Lieut. William Ingraham whom we have mentioned as being killed in the service.

Capt. D. N. Ingraham received his Midshipman's warrant at the age of nine years, on the 18th of June, 1812, during our last war with Great Britain. Commodore Smith, of South Carolina, the intimate friend of his father, being about to sail in the frigate Congress, requested Mr. Ingraham to allow him to take his son with him. "We shall probably have an engagement," said he, "and it will do him good." He accordingly went to sea at once, at that tender age, and remained in active service for two years, until the close of the war. He then returned home at the age of eleven, and resumed his education at school. Since then he has most of the time been employed in active duty. He commanded the ill-fated Somers in the blockade duty at Vera Cruz and other parts of the Gulf during the whole of the Mexican war, and being prostrated by sickness, was sent home but a short time before she was lost. For two years previous to his sailing for the Mediterranean, in the St. Louis, he was attached to the Navy Yard at Philadelphia, the society of which city will long remember him and his accomplished family.

He was in command of the St. Louis in 1853 in the harbor of Smyrna, when he made his name so famous in connection with the Costa exploit while at that port. He bearded the lion in his den, demanding and obtaining from the Austrian Government the release of Costa as an American citizen. On the 15th of September, 1855, he was promoted to a Captaincy, and after an interval of inactivity was, on the 10th of March, 1856, attached to the Bureau of Ordnance as its Chief. He held this position at a salary of $3,500 a year when the rebellion broke out, when he, like many other traitors, forsook the flag under which he had so long fought and through which he had received many honors, to join the cause of the rebels.

Captain Ingraham married Harriet Rutledge Laurens of South Carolina, a grand-daughter, on the paternal side, of Henry Laurens, the President of the first Continental Congress, and who afterwards was captured by a British frigate while on his way to France as American Commissioner, and confined for a long time in the Tower of London. On the maternal side she is the grand-daughter of Edward Rutledge, one of the signers of the Declaration of Independence. His eldest son, Henry Laurens Ingraham, was a Lieutenant of the Marine Corps when the rebellion broke out.

It is a curious circumstance, that by intermarriage with the American family, the Ingraham blood flows in the veins of some of the most distinguished officers of the British Navy. Among those was the late Captain Marryatt, C. B., (the author,) and Sir Edward Belcher, K. C. B., who commanded the exploring expedition round the world, and who in 1853 commanded the Arctic expedition, sent out by the British Admiralty, in search of Sir John Franklin. The grand-mother of both these officers was an Ingraham, the near relative of Commodore Ingraham.

As a *resume*, it may be as well to state that he was in the United States service nearly fifty years, fourteen of which were spent at sea, nine on shore and other duty, and the remainder unemployed, although receiving pay. More than half his time he accepted the pay of the United States for doing nothing else than seeking the best means to ruin and betray her.

SKETCH OF CAPTAIN RUTLEDGE.

The rebel Captain John Rutledge was formerly an officer in the United States Navy. He is a native and citizen of South Carolina, from which State he was appointed to the navy on the 9th of April, 1835. On the 21st of June, 1841, he was warranted as a Past Midshipman, and on the 7th of January, 1849, was promoted to a Lieutenancy, which rank he held when the rebellion broke out. Up to that time he has been nearly twenty six years in the United States service, eighteen years of which has been spent at sea, three on shore and other duty, and the remainder unemployed. He has seen a fair amount of service under the stars and stripes, and has now warred upon that flag which had protected him, and which he has so disgraced.

Charleston Courier, February, 1862.

THE UNITED STATES AND CONFEDERATE NAVAL FORCES.

The naval forces of the Confederate States and France compared with the navy of the *defunct United States*. A significant comparison, inasmuch as it was made by a presumptuous Yankee. Partial admission of blockades having been raised by the growing power of the Confederate navy forces.

H. W. R. J.

A writer in the New York "Sunday Mercury," of February 22, in calling attention to the threatened conflict between the United States and France, sums up the total number of vessels of the French navy at four hundred and eighty-nine, including six formidable iron-cased frigates and fourteen iron-plated batteries. This immense force, he says, would be used against the United States in connection with the Confederates. He says:

At the outset of hostilities between Napoleon III, and the Federal Government, the latter would be found the poorer prepared for them—being vulnerable at a dozen different points between Portland and New Orleans. Our blockading fleet, too, would have fearful odds to contend with should the Imperial will offer to enter the sealed ports of the Southern States. We possess all the national defences, and must protect all except those located at four points, viz: Wilmington, Charleston, Mobile and Galveston. Where his Majesty would first show his hostile colors is a matter beyond conjecture; consequently, provision to meet him at all points is imperatively demanded. Still, there is hope for us in the future, as may be discovered from reflection upon the character which the war would assume, and our resources in men and ships. The main difficulty in engaging in the contest would arise from our deficiency in ordnance. We must meet this want, however, and we therefore proceed to show what we may do presuming the necessary provision to have been made.

The navy of the United States is rapidly increasing, and, in the right direction. We find the following list of iron-clads afloat, or near completion:

Agamentious, Benton, Baron DeKalb, Chillicothe, Chickasaw, Catskill, Camanche, Cairo, Caroudelet, Circinnati, Canonicus, Catawba, Dictator, Dunderberg, Essex, Galena, Keokuk (Moodna,) Kickapoo, Lexington, Lehigh, Louisville, Monoduck, Marctta, Manhattan, Mahopac, Moynayunk, Miantonomah, Milwaukie, Montauk, Nantucket, Nahant, Neosho, New Ironsides, Ozark, Osage, Onondaga, Patapsco, Passaic, Puritan, Pittsburg, Roanoke, Sandusky, Sangamon, Wehawken, Winnebago.

RAM GUNBOATS AND BATTERIES AFLOAT, OR NEAR COMPLETION.

General Bragg, General Price, General Pillow, Lioness, Queen of the West, Switzerland, Lafayette, Little Rebel, Sampson.

Making a grand total of the iron-clad fleet, soon to be ready, 54 vessels. The Puritan and Dictator are designated to be peculiarly formidable. They measure over 8,000 tons, are to be armed with ordnance capable of throwing a two ton shot, and will be provided with exceedingly sharp and strong prows.

With those now building, the total estimate of our naval force, including transports and receiving ships, is set down at 390 vessels.

THE CONFEDERATE NAVAL FORCE.

The Confederate Navy is also a rapidly growing power. On the ocean, already, the rebel mark has been made by the Alabama, Captain Semmes; the Oreto (Florida,) Captain Newland Maffit (son of the famous Methodist preacher,) and the Retribution, Captain's name unknown. In Charleston harbor there are three iron-clads, steamers of course, the Palmetto State, Captain Rutledge, Chicora, Captain Tucker, and City of Charleston; besides three or four more small steamers, such as the General Clinch, Etiwan and Chesterfield, and the celebrated floating battery which did such effective execution during the Fort Sumter bombardment. At Richmond, Merrimac No. 2 is supposed to be watching a favorable opportunity for coming out. Our Government constantly keeps a blockading fleet of one iron-clad and a dozen old style war vessels at the mouth of the James River to prevent her escape, which looks as if she were rated a pretty dangerous adversary. There is also the City of Richmond, her consort, penned in. At Savannah the ram Fingal lies *perdu*. She is supposed to be a magnificent craft, very powerfully armed, and was altered from an English vessel of superior build. The Nashville has done, and may yet render, signal service to the rebels. The Thunderbolt is a superior vessel, now being built. At Mobile there are said to be three iron-clad gunboats under way, that are to be provided with the best Whitworth, Blakeley and Armstrong guns. The Sumter is still an object of Federal attention at Gibraltar, where we kept a "spotter" in constant attendance. The Harriet Lane is now in the hands of the enemy. Besides these vessels, the rebels have two or three efficient musquito fleets in the Gulf harbors, and some effective batteries and rams, good in helping to raise blockades, or disposing the entrance of light gunboats.

To recapitulate the Confederate maritime strength, we find that they possess:

Cruisers, 4; Iron-clads, 8; Rams, 2; Gunboats and transports, 5; Harbor fleets, of say, 25. Total 44.

WHERE NAPOLEON WOULD FIGHT US, AND HOW.

It is evident that were he to undertake hostilities against us it would be in the interest of the Confederate States, and that he would, with their assistance, raise the blockade and land troops in different portions of their rebellious territory. Again, these we could readily fight—not one but two millions of men, or even more could doubtless be had to sustain the Government against the double foe.

The North would unite without delay—political grievances would be again buried, as they were after the first gun at Sumter, and Napoleon would find himself the cause of the speedy and sure overthrow of the Confederacy, which he would be fighting to sustain. But at sea his power might afford us more apprehension; and self-defence would compel us to swarm the Atlantic with privateers. The conflict would be desperate in character; and, undoubtedly, completely stagnate the commerce of both countries. But France could never enter our harbors except with lighter draught vessels than those she is now building, unless in rare cases. Light gunboats alone could cross our bars, and what could be done to check their progress and eventually conquer them, besides opposing similar vessels to them, has been shown in our suggestions about the proper mode of defending New York. In the use of cruisers we should find ourselves able to do more damage along the hostile coast, and and in the very ports of France, than we would be likely to be called upon to sustain ourselves from the nature of the contest. The Apostle of the Latin race, as he is now religiously termed, would do well to weigh the case carefully before entering into active alliance with the bastard Government at Richmond, and making common cause with it against a Republic whose recuperative powers and unceasing energy has been the wonder and admiration of European nations in an especial manner during the last two years.

ENGLAND'S POSITION IN THE EVENT OF THE STRUGGLE.

The policy which England would be apt to pursue, in the event of her taking up arms against France, is almost beyond fathom. That she would rejoice at our accumulating troubles, is a matter of course; but whether she would seek to profit by the opportunity in a manner other than by endeavoring to make money in bestowing aid and material to all parties as long as she could, is a point that cannot yet be discussed. Possibly she would deem the time come for her to strike that cherished blow at her dangerous rival, of which we have heard so much, and would place herself on our side for the purpose. This would involve the whole world in the most tremendous conflict ever waged, and lead to an unheard of amount of desolation on both continents. But sound judgment must argue strongly against her adopting any course but that which she has found to pay so well, and which goes by the name of "strict neutrality."

Our enemy in the above account, dated February 22, 1863, of naval forces, has not given us credit for four or five of the most formidable gunboats we have recently captured out of his would-be all-powerful navy; among them are the Queen of the West, Indianola, Isaac Smith and several others. The Harriet Lane is the only one spoken of in the above account as being in our possession. Seven ot eight of the enemies gunboats have been sunk in attempting to pass the batteries at Vicksburg during the past two months, among which are several of the formidable iron-clads mentioned in the above list, to wit: the Benton, Cincinnati, Galena, Montauk, &c. During the past few months we have captured and sunk more gunboats and iron-clads than the enemy could possibly build in twice the length of time that was required for us to capture and destroy them.

H. W. R. J.

The blockade on the coast of Texas has been raised, January, 1863, by Major General Magruder, who immediately issued a proclamation declaring that as the ports of Sabine Pass, Lavaca and Velasco, on the coast of Texas, have ceased to be actually blockaded by the forced withdrawal of the enemy's fleet from the same, he invites friendly neutral nations to resume commercial intercourse with these ports until an actual blockade has been re-established with the usual notice demanded by the laws of nations.

A DUTY PARAMOUNT TO EVERY CONSIDERATION OF PROFIT—AN APPEAL TO RAISE BREADSTUFFS.

A wise man may learn not only from a fool, but from his enemy, and nations may act upon and derive benefit from the same principle. With this object in view, we give below an appeal to Northern and Western farmers, from the pen of one of them who evidently sees breakers ahead of the section, to "Plant Corn." Our planters and small farmers may everywhere benefit by it, and we trust they will. They hardly realize the advantage they possess over the North in producing breadstuffs. There the farmers can make but a single crop of anything upon the same ground, and it must all be planted within a given, and very brief period, or the early frosts will kill it. How different with the agriculturists of the South! They may plant some kind of food-producing crops during almost any month of the year.

Hitherto, very little attention, comparitively, has been given to this subject, planters depending in many instances, almost entirely upon the West for their provisions, and others to a greater or less extent. All this, however, must now be changed, and the Southern States must rely wholly upon themselves for their food. Fortunately, they have all the means to be desired at their disposal. They have only to put forth their hands and plant, and eat and live. They have the acres, the genial climate, and the labor necessary to the production of almost every kind of corn, grain, vegetable, and fruit that enters into the composition of human food. Let the people be alive to the great fact, and avail themselves of their advantages. Let them plant, plant, plant. Their soil, though not inexhaustible, is rich, and may be made richer by care and industry. Plow up the old fields, and plow deep, the deeper the better, and plant corn, potatoes, beans, peas, etc., and see by a proper variation of the kinds of seed, a succession of crops is produced. Any quantity of white potatoes can be grown so as to mature in the fall—a circumstance whose importance has been overlooked hitherto. Late corn may also be planted, as well as sweet potatoes, a most valuable root. But listen to the following importunately earnest and touching cry, though tinged with the prevailing fanaticism, to "plant corn," addressed to Northern farmers, or rather their wives and children, by an agricultural journal, and then let all of our planters and farmers profit by the appeal.

"Plant Corn."—It is the duty of those who take arms in their hands to drive back the foe, to provide for that danger. It is the duty of those who stay at home to provide against the danger of short crops. In short to provide that they are as abundant as industrious labor, judiciously and economically directed, can possibly effect. To do this, we must begin now. Now is the seed time, let us do our duty, and trust God for the harvest. Brother farmers, we urge you to plant corn. Plow deep, manure well, and plant corn.

American mothers, wives, and daughters of American soldiers, we urge you to plant corn.

What if every woman, who has the ability, shall plant and tend one well-fertilized hill of corn?

Who can imagine the vast addition all the golden ears grown upon these extra stalks would make to the great national store?

What if they were all garnered in one garner, and added to the widows and orphans fund?

Think of this, mothers, wives and daughters. Think what you can do with such a trifling addition to your other labors as planting one hill of corn.

"Only three grains of corn, mother," let every child cry, in all the month of May, and plant it, and then follow the Scriptural injunction,. "Dig about it and dung it, until it grows and bears fruit."

The waste bones of a single dinner, burned and pulverized, will more than fertilize a hill of corn. The sweepings, the slops, the pieces of a small family, mixed in a tub, and carefully applied as a liquid manure, would fertilize a hundred hills of corn; aye, more, would add a hundred bushels to the crop. Then plant "three grains of corn." Dig the soil deep and mellow. Soak the seed to hasten its vegetation. Keep the ground free of weeds, and the surface loose, and moist, and rich. Dig in the early morning dew. There is no better fertilizer. If you plant the right kind, three grains will produce six ears, and each of these will have a hundred grains.

Men, women, and children—all who love your country—all who have a superficial foot of the surface of the country—we ask you to plant one hill of corn. Thus you can save your country in its hour of peril. You can with your feeble hands alone, provide a surplus of grain. Seeing your spirit, your strong handed relatives will be animated to renewed and greater exertion, and each and all, throughout all the corn-growing region of States, unpolluted with slavery, will plant one more hill of corn."

To carry on this fanatical and brutal war, which demagogues have inaugurated against the South, the wives and children of Northern and Western farmers are thus adjured to go out into the fields and toil, to plant "one hill of corn." This shows to what terrible straits the demagogues feel they have reduced their section of the country. To ward off a famine, actual starvation, they appeal to women and children to turn themselves into workmen, and dig and sweat, that the politicians may enjoy office and cormorants fatten upon the common miseries. For this there will come a reckoning day; but let us inaugurate the policy of entire home independence in the department of breadstuffs when it can be so easily done, with work comparatively so light, and harvests so sure, so abundant, and so important.

Vast amounts of fertilizers might be saved upon every plantation by the requisite pains and forethought, and turned to the enriching of the soil, and the consequent increase of crops. Millions of dollars are every year lost to the South in this way—from sheer neglect and improvidence. We trust to see a speedy reform in this respect, and a great increase of all kinds of cereals, fruits, and vegetables, as the natural result of it. Less cotton and more food should be the motto, till the end of the war, whether it be one year or ten.

Fruits will soon be ripe, and many a patriotic housewife in the South may make all her pin money by putting them up in hermetrically sealed cans for the New Orleans and other markets.—*New Orleans Bulletin, May 1862.*

THE APPEAL OF THE ALABAMA DELEGATION

The Confederate Senators and Representatives from Alabama have issued a very patriotic appeal to the planters of that

State, urging them to raise everything 'in their power in the eating line. The Honorable gentlemen say.:

The raising the present year of the largest possible quantity of provisions, and the raising of pork, beef and mutton for the supply of the army and the support of the people, have become manifestly the duty of every citizen. The enemy have possession of some portion of our country well adapted to raising provisions. In other portions when in the possession of the enemy, they have damaged farms, houses, and fences, plundered and appropriated stock, and destroyed farming implements, under a hope that if they could not conquer us by arms, they could subjugate us with the aid of starvation.

It behooves us, therefore, so to provide as to satify our enemies that they are not to have the aid of short crops, and consequent want and suffering, in their wicked attempts to subjugate, rob and plunder us. We have the soil and the labor, if properly used, to raise provisions and supplies in abundance. We urge you and each of you, in the present state of affairs, to devote the soil and the labor at your command to the planting and cultivation of provision crops, such as corn, peas, potatoes, and vegetables of all kinds; and that you raise pork and beef, so that our gallant army may be liberally fed, the people have abundance, and our servants be saved from want and suffering, such as has been the fate of those who have fallen into the hands of the enemy, left to decay, starvation and neglect.

Every cultivator of the soil is deeply interested in expelling from our lines the invaders of our homes, and this can only be done by raising supplies sufficient for the liberal support of all. Our true policy is to cultivate no cotton except to a small extent for home consumption, and devote the labor of the country to the raising of provisions.

PLANTING AND FARMING HINTS.

The Agricultural Editor of the "Southern Field and Fireside, who presides over a valuable department of a most valuable and deserving organ, writes:

"Good seed Corn on poor land will make a better yield than snebbins on rich soil." Land that will not produce more than ten bushels to the acre is hardly worth planting. Better plant less and manure well.

"Of Sweet Potatoes, the Yam is the best for the table, the Alabama and Spanish for stock feeding—should be planted early in March.

"Of Peas, the 'Yellow Speckled' or 'Whippoorwill,' is very productive but yields little forage. The 'Small Yellow' is recommended where the vine is wanted. The Jerusalem Artichoke, Chufa and Ground Pea, should be planted freely for hogs. The *Colza* (*Branica lacinati*) is strongly commended as an oil plant."

SPARE THE GARDENS.

The Richmond "Dispatch" says: "In every place where our armies are stationed commanding officers should exercise the strictest discipline in preventing injury to private property, either to fencing, fruits, vegetables, or animals. We are aware of the law-and-order-loving character of our soldiers, but there are others who are not to be restrained from depredations except by strict discipline. At this time, when every foot of ground ought to be cultivated, and when a full supply of garden vegetables may relieve in some measure the deficiency of meat, the greatest care should be taken by the military and civil authorities to encourage the cultivation of the soil. No gardens at all will be made in the neighborhood of large armies unless they are secured from depredation."

We regret to state that reckless and wanton depredations have been committed against farms and gardens in this vicinity. These disorders, we believe, are committed by very few soldiers or persons wearing the badges of soldiers.

The general reputation of most of our brave soldiers is as good for order and civil deportment as for gallantry in action. It is the interest of all good and orderly soldiers that the depredations and misdeeds of those who bring the service into ill repute and who threaten to interfere with the supply of provisions from our farms, should be detected and exemplary punished.

Where officers do their duty, soldiers are never dangerous or destructive to their friends.

HOME MEDICINES—THE POPPY FOR OPIUM.

It will be most profitable, and render vast service to the country. If any of you have Poppy Seed to spare, send them to Dr. Blaskie; he will distribute them.

We also urge upon every family to raise large quantities of pepper, sage, balm, thyme, &c., &c. It is all wanted.

"FAMINE IN THE SOUTH"

Under this suggestive head, a number of the papers of the North are endeavoring to show to their readers that the "rebellion" may soon be brought to a close by the appearance of starvation in the Confederacy. They are impressed with the idea that the people and the army are already suffering from want of food, and believe that if they can before many weeks succeed in obtaining possession of the seaports of the country, and continue to hold the country at present under their control, the "rebels" will be compelled to submit or starve.

The other day, when Yankee prisoners were passing through Knoxville, their officers in conversation frankly confessed that they did not believe that the South could be conquered by the sword, but were perfectly confident that the rebellion would be *starved out* in a year more.

THE CHEAPEST FOOD.

The cheapest and most nutritious vegetable used for food is beans. Prof. Liebig says that pork and beans form a compound of substances peculiarly adapted to furnish all that is necessary to support life. A quart of beans and half a pound of pork will feed a small family for a day with good strengthening food. Four quarts of beans and two pounds of corned beef, boiled to rags, in fifty quarts of water, will furnish a good meal for forty men.—*Charleston Courier*, 1863.

SOMETHING TO BE DONE.

One of the greatest wants of the medical department, says the "South Carolinian," is opium and its preparations. The poppy, its source, is within our reach. The common garden poppy is easily cultivated, and all we want is for the ladies to take it in hand. The only preparation needed is to slice the capsules and collect the juice on plates or glass, and to dry it and forward it to the nearest medical purveyor. He will prepare it for use. Will not our women take this in hand in their flower gardens? It is specially their province to soothe suffering and solace the distressed. Let them take the matter up and the fall season will show an immense supply of the most valuable medicine that the army needs.

A MODEL BOY.

A correspondent of the Mobile "Advertiser and Register" writes from Savannah:

This allusion to the "Republican" reminds me of the wonderful success which has attended the efforts of one of the boys engaged in the sale of that paper in the camps around the city. Within a period of eighteen months he accumulated money enough to purchase a horse and dray, but finding that he was too small to load and unload his dray, he sold it and the horse, and invested the money in five milch cows. He still continues to furnish the paper to the soldiers, and with the profits arising from the sale he buys feed for his cows. The income arising from the sale of papers and the milk given by his cows, is now ten dollars a day, or at the rate of about $3500 per annum. This boy will make his way in the world, and I allude to his good fortune that the boys engaged in the sale of the "Advertiser and Register" may take heart and emulate his example. You may tell your boys that this Savannah boy does not swear, nor use tobacco, nor drink liquor, but loves his mother and is very industrious.

One of Major-General J. E. B. Stuart's servants is in captivity, glorifying in his Southern proclivities, and declaring that he will "die fuss 'fore he'll take the oaf of allegiance." The same darkey, the morning after the passage of the negro regiment bill, told his fellow prisoners that the white men of the North had found themselves unable to whip the Southern Confederacy, and had to call on the "niggers."

GEN. PILLOW AND THE PRESIDENT.

Gen. Pillow recently made a speech to Planters in Alabama, to induce them to permit their slaves to enter Government employ as teamsters, etc. To show that he was not asking them to make sacrifices that he himself would not make, he told of his own losses—400 negroes, four gin houses worth $10,000 each, 100,000 pounds of bacon, 2000 hogs, 500 head of cattle, his houses and plantations destroyed and desolated, and 2100 bales of his cotton burned by his own Government.

He stated that Gen. Sherman had written him a letter, couched in very polite language, offering to return his negroes to him, and to indemnify him for all his losses, if he would abandon the Confederate service. His answer was:

General, whilst I thank you for your courteous letter, let me say to you, the property your Government has taken from me was my own. Your Government has the power to rob me of it, but it is too poor to buy me." Concerning President Davis, he said: "The President is the very man for the position he holds; if he cannot conduct us through this revolution, no man could; he is a man of delicate form, but of large brain and patriotic heart, and eminently qualified in every respect for the Chief Executive of the Confederacy." Although he thought the President had not done him justice, yet he preferred him for President to any other man. We were not now fighting for President Davis, nor for any other man, but for our rights as freemen; and as for himself he would, if he had it to do over, vote for Jefferson Davis for President, if he knew that he would place him in a dungeon during the whole war.

The "Southern Christian Advocate" says such remarks evince a noble and unselfish patriotism, that sets the country above self, and we take pleasure in recording them and recommending them to the notice of whatever selfish churl may be looking to his own gain honors, rather than to his country's weal.—*Charleston Courier.*

STAMPEDE OF CONTRABAND TROOPS.

A correspondent of the Hartford (Connecticut) "Times" writes from Hilton Head, Feb. 2:

The negro expedition from St. Mary's has just returned. It was composed of four companies of the negro regiments. They went after negro recruits and lumber. They got together a lot of negroes, but they refused to come away and were left behind. They did not succeed in getting any lumber. The transports were fired at from the shores. Captain Jack Clifton, of the steamer John Adams, was killed by a ball through the head. He was well known all over New York. He was the brother of the celebrated actress, Josephine Clifton, and was very much liked for his social and cheerful qualities. His wife and daughter are at Beaufort. His loss is regretted by all. The The expedition succeeded in bringing off four non-combatants. The town of St. Mary's was burned by the negroes.

The negroes landed and encamped at St. Mary's. During the night twenty rebels on horseback made a dash into their camp, when the negroes fled in every direction, and then stampeded for the transports, throwing away their guns. They rushed pell-mell on board, and created the greatest confusion. The rebels fired from high bluffs, and our troops could not elevate their guns enough to do much execution.

A VALUABLE SUGGESTION TO PLANTERS.

A correspondent of the "Savannah News" suggests to planters that they prepare to plant largely of slip or layer of sweet potatoes. He says:

There is now ample time for the preparation as they may be planted as late as the latter part of July and produce a good crop. I have made 350 bushels per acre on very light land, by the application of about two bushels of rough stable manure to the task row, and much larger yields have been made to my knowledge; but if only 50 bushels were made it will be a good return for the labor required.

As an article of food I need not say much, as their properties are well known; but as I am convinced that they have never been properly appreciated as food for horses, I wish to make known the fact that they are equal to corn or oats in quality, and I think 5 pecks of potatoes equal to 4 of corn for horses; at least my experience for several years justifies my conclusion. They should not be fed to horses until they have been banked about three weeks, as they are apt to give the soours; but after that there is no danger. Simply let them be dry and not wasted, and no danger need be apprehended. As the cost of transportation would be greater than corn, I would suggest that farmers use them at home and ship their corn to points where it may be needed.

PATRIOTISM OF NEGROES—THE OLD DRUMMER OF CHALMETTE.

The old negro drummer, Jordan, of historic fame as a drummer at the battle of New Orleans, in conformity with the order of Beast Butler, handed in a complete list of his property for confiscation by the Lincoln government, and 'declared himself "an enemy of the United States." The Louisiana "Democrat" says:

Ten thousand of those citizens of New Orleans pretending to be loyal, who have sworn allegiance to the United States, for the purpose of saving their property, must have blushed from shame when they saw this old negro voluntarily stripping himself of his hard-earned gains, and becoming penniless in the evening of his days, rather than yield obedience to a Government which has become an object of the contempt of the civilized world.—*November*, 1862.

NEGRO PATRIOTISM.

Benjamin Marrable, Esq., of Halifax county, Virginia, has four negro men who, for some time, have been engaged working on the fortifications at Richmond. A few days ago they came up home on a visit, and finding good warm clothing, excellent shoes and socks made for them, they generously declined them, on condition that their master would send them to the suffering soldiers who, they said, needed them much more than they did. They had seen suffering soldiers, and it touched their hearts to compassion, besides they want the South to conquer. Now, how many miserable money grabbers and Shylocks, with white skin, but with hearts blacker than the hides of these contrabands, would have been as self-sacrificing, generous and magnanimous? Not one! The articles thus contributed by these colored men would buy several barrels of corn, at the extortioner's price. Let many "white" men think of this.

Milton Chronicle, 1862

A LOYAL NEGRO.

A correspondent informs us that a committee was recently appointed in Portsmouth to urge Robert Butt, a negro of that place, of worthy repute, and who rendered himself famous for his kindness during the prevalence of the yellow fever, to become a candidate for Congress to represent that District. The negro, more loyal than Segar or Cowper, promptly sent the following response, which our correspondent assures us was copied from the original.—*Richmond Enquirer*.

PORTSMOUTH, December 22, 1862.
To John Council, John O. Lawrence, Nicholas Butler and others, Committee:

Gents—Accept my grateful ack owledgments for your flattering invitation to become a candidate to represent the District in the 37th Congress of the United States

There was a day in the history of our once glorious country, when such an invitation would have been received with some consideration, but now things are very different, and to accept such a position when I know, if elected, I cannot represent the voice of the people of this District. In my humble opinion, gentlemen, any individual who would suffer his name to be used in this connection, and under the existing circumstances, would disgrace himself, and show but little respect for his friends of the District who are beyond the lines of the United States Government, fighting for our very existence. I must decline your invitation to become a candidate (to be voted for by ballot) for a seat in a Congress which knows no law, except the higher law, and are every day enacting unconstitutional measures, thereby disgracing the capital of the country. No, gentlemen; I will leave this position to some one who is more anxious to act the traitor, and have his name written high upon the page of infamy, than one who has ever borne within his bosom the true motto of his mother State—"Down with the tyrant."

I am, gentlemen, very respectfully,
your obedient, humble servant,
ROBERT BUTT.

From the New York World.
THE MURDER OF THE BLACK RACE.

The "Evening Post" frankly admits that the ultimate object of the radicals is the destruction of the colored race on this continent. It says:

"As the Indians were crowded westward, and out of our bounds, by the irresistible advance of the white man, so will the blacks be whenever that powerful protective system with which the slaveholders have guarded them is removed. It is the destiny of the free white working men of this country to possess it; the efforts of the slaveholders have hitherto robbed them of one-half of it—the richest, fairest half—and devoted it to the blacks. It is the slaveholders who have preserved the negro from decline among us; it is the slaveholders who have increased the blacks from seven hundred thousand in 1790 to four millions in 1860."

So it is admitted that those terrible fellows, the slaveholders, whose chains, whips and blood-hounds we have heard so much about in anti-slavery novels and poems, are after all the real conservators of the negro race, while the Abolitionists, with all their professions of philanthropy, contemplate their destruction. The "Post" is right. The freeing of negroes means their extinction as a race in North America; the history of the present war proves that, beyond all peradventure. From Arkansas around to Port Royal the same complaint reaches us, that the negroes within our army lines are in rags and starving, and that the soldiers abuse and hate them. A card in yesterday's "Tribune," from the agents of some negro missionary society, begging for money and clothes, says:

"There are about a thousand in Hampton, quartered in tents, and a still larger number at Norfolk—seven hundred and eighty at Norfolk, and three hundred and seventy quartered in a large storehouse and in barracks. Could the benevolent look upon these pitiable objects of charity, tattered and shoeless, destitute of decent clothing, and compelled to sleep on hard boards, bricks or ground, without a pallet, or hardly a rag under them, their hearts would bleed, and 'eyes unused to weep o'erflow with tears.'

"It is not improbable that there are sixty thousand freed negro families within our lines in this condition, and, under the operation of the emancipation proclamation, as our army advances, this number will double and treble. These poor people are destined for misery and ultimate destruction. The North— even Massachusetts—will not allow them a residence, and for the present, perhaps for years, there can be no fixed system of labor where they are located."

What a strange verdict will history pass upon the Abolition party. It was originally organized to champion the woes of the black race; it made the world ring with the alleged cruelties of the slaveholders; yet this same party, in less than two years after it assumed power, inflicted more real distress upon the black race than have several generations of slaveholders. More than that, one of its principal organs now admits that the negroes thrive under the sway of slaveholders, but are destined to perish from out the land at the expense of their quondam friends, the Abolitionists.

NO LOVE FOR SAMBO—NEGROES EXPELLED FROM INDIANA.

The City Council of Vincennes, Indiana, adopted on the 6th instant the following preamble and resolution:

WHEREAS, a number of negroes were brought into the country on the 1st inst., on the Ohio and Mississippi Railroad, from the vicinity of Noble, Indiana, from which point they were forwarded, as we learn by a man named Hughes, who had procured them at Cairo to work on his farm; and whereas, the presence of said negroes among us is contrary to the laws and constitution of the State of Indiana; therefore,

Resolved, That the Mayor, with the assistance of the City Marshal and such other forces as may be necessary, be required to take immediate steps toward having said negroes sent back from whence they came, consigned to the party or parties who forwarded them to this point, if, upon consultation with the City Attorney, it is determined that such action can be legally taken; and that, in the meantime, all parties employing the negroes aforesaid, or any other negroes, in our city or county, contrary to the constitution and laws of the State, be proceeded against at once.

The condition of these negroes is said to be deplorable. They are crowded together in a ruinous building in the outskirts of the town. One of them has died, and others are sick.

Confederacy, November, 1862.

THE NEGROES TO BE FORCED TO FIGHT.

The Washington "Chronicle" lays down the law for the negroes thus: Fighting promiscuous is forbid, and they must go in the forefront of the battle. The Yankees evidently intend to destroy the entire breed in America.

General Hunter believes the employment of blacks as soldiers to be necessary to the preservation of our country. The result of the war must be to secure to them the inestimable blessing which, but for the rebellion, could never have been attained by the present, or, perhaps, the next generation. This being the case, it is no more than fair that negroes should aid us in crushing that rebellion which is as hostile to their interests as it is to ours; and if there are among them any who are too selfish or two cowardly to make sacrifices and incur risks for the sake of the great privilege of their manhood, they should be compelled to do their duty.

ONE YANKEE AND THREE NEGROES BURIED IN ONE HOLE.

On White River there is a grave in which are buried a white man, a negro woman and two negro men. In one of the battles last year, among the killed were the chaplain of the 1st Wisconsin regiment, who had shortly before married a negro wench, the property of a Mr. Thomas, and the negroes also. When our troops came to bury the dead, they put the parson and his wife in the hole, and, to give him enough of nigger company, threw in the bodies of two negro men, who had been killed in the action.—*Little Rock Democrat.*

THE NEGRO BEGINS TO "HURT" IN MASSACHUSETTS.

The backs of the Yankees are becoming sore under the negro saddle which they voluntarily begirted themselves with, and they have already commenced wincing under the self-assumed burden even in negro-worshiping Massachusetts. The Boston "Courier," of March 16th, lets loose a winning half-suppressed complaint, which we copy:

THE DIFFERENCE.—About a week ago several persons, and among them one or more officers, having been condemned by a court martial held at the Navy Yard, were quietly taken to the State prison at Charlestown, shaved, clad in prison costume and put to hard labor. We announce this fact thus nakedly without approval or condemnation, for the consideration of the people of the Commonwealth. In times past, when under the laws of the United States fugitive slaves, were arrested in Massachusetts, the use of the State prisons and the help of the State officers were denied to the General Government by statute. What has so changed matters, that while the Government may not be aided as to one class of persons it may be as to another? Is it not clear that both cases cannot be right? If so, which is wrong?—*March*, 1863.

A FULL YANKEE LIEUTENANT A NEGRO.

Yesterday a lot of some ten or twelve prisoners—mostly bushwhackers—captured near the Big Creek Gap by Colonel Palmer's command, were brought to this city. Among them was a negro, named John Edmonds, who claimed to be a regularly commissioned Federal Lieutenant. He states that he started out as cook in the 33d Indiana regiment, but on their retreat, from Cumberland Gap, was left in the mountains. He subsequently joined Capt. Goodwin's company of bushwhackers, in which he was commissioned a Lieutenant, sleeping and messing with the white officers. He boasts of having killed three "secesh" with his own hand. The guard who escorted him to jail could scarce refrain from lynching him at this avowal, and only the doubt as to whether he was *compos mentis* saved his black hide. He professes to own $9,000 worth of property in Indiana, and says he could have had a white wife there if he had wanted one; and that his commission as a Lieutenant is at Captain Goodwin's house.

In addition to the above, some thirty to forty other prisoners were brought before Provost Marshal Toole, consisting of deserters, renegades, bushwhackers, &c.—*Knoxville Register, 7th.*

THE NEGRO IN THIS WAR.

"P. W. A.," writing to the Mobile "Advertiser," from Savannah, says:

The negro is performing an important part in the great work of our redemption. At one of the foundries to-day, I saw a number of blacks engaged upon the monster shells and parrot balls. At another place several were at work upon a species of machinery which must be nameless. Beyond the city, both on water and land, they have rendered important services in the construction of the fortifications which environ the town. This is all right. No one has a deeper interest in the success of the Confederate arms than the negro. Every blow he strikes—every bolt he forges—is a blow and a bolt in his own behalf. The success of the North would be the ruin of the black man. It would reduce him to rags, to starvation, to death. The success of the South, on the contrary, would perpetuate the happy condition he now occupies in our beneficent social system—a state of comfort and civilization to which the sons of Ham have attained in no other part of the world. Well may the negro assist, therefore, in the erection of batteries and the forging of the thunderbolts of war. It is for himself that he works.

CRIME AND ITS PUNISHMENT.

A Northern paper publishes the following item:

A letter from a correspondent at Denton in Maryland, gives the details of a terrible tragedy enacted at that place on Saturday last. A mulatto man named Jim Wilson had outraged and murdered a little daughter of Edgar Plummer, about 11 years of age, residing near Brighton, in Carolina county, meeting her in the woods on her way from school. The perpetrator of this terrible outrage was arrested, confessed the deed, and was committed to the Denton jail. The people of the surrounding country flocked to the town and broke open the jail, took out the prisoner, hung him to a tree, fired sixteen bullets into the body, dragged it through the streets attached to the rope, put it up, burned it, and concluded the ceremony by giving three cheers for Stonewall Jackson.—*November*, 1862.

THE KEY TO THE PROSPERITY OF THE CONFEDERACY.

"Kin you tell me, Sambo, de key to de prosperity of de Souf?"

"Key to prosperity of de Souf? Big words, Juno; guess you must hab been eating massa's dickshunary. Golly, I ain't learned nuff to answer dat."

"Well, chile 'tis de dark ey."—*Field and Fireside.*

THE NEGRO AND THE YANKEE—THE YANKEE HANGS THE NEGRO—AND HIS OPINION OF HIM.

In a series of letters from correspondents of New York and Philadelphia journals attached to the Federal army in the Peninsula. They were dated in New Kent county. One of them, dated at New Kent C. H., May 13th, has the following paragraph, which we think worthy of special attention:

"A negro, a very desperate character, was hung at West

Point, on the river, last Friday, for the cold-blooded murder of two Massachusetts soldiers. He had caught them asleep alone, and murdered them for their money. He was caught the next day, and was made to jump off the limb of a tree with a rope around his neck. This murder, and other instances of atrocity, cruelty, deceit and ingratitude, on the part of negroes in camp, have completely cured the Massachusetts soldiers of that negro worshipping mania of which they have hitherto been possessed. They have repeatedly declared, in my hearing, that they wished that the war could be conducted in such a manner as would leave the status of slavery just as it was before the war; for the slaves have proved themselves utterly unworthy of freedom, and utterly unfit to be free. And such, too, have been my experience in regard to them.—1862.

DERIVATION AND MEANING OF THE WORD YANKEE.

The Richmond "Whig" has discovered in a record of travel kept by one Thomas Anburey, and published in London in 1791, the following in reference to the derivation and meaning of the word Yankee. Having referred to the New Englanders as Yankees, he says:

"*Apropos*—It may not be amiss just here to observe to you the etymology of this term. It is derived from a Cherokee word, *eunkke*, which signifies coward and slave. This epithet of Yankee was bestowed upon the inhabitants of New England by the Virginians, for not assisting them in a war with the Cherokees, and they have always been held in derision by it."

NEW SLAVE TRADE.

A gentleman direct from Alexandria, Virginia, where the Yankees have possession, informs us that two vessels left that port one day last week loaded with slaves stolen from the loyal citizens of Virginia, and doubtless bound for St. Croix, or some other West India Island. A vessel recently sailed from the York river, where she arrived a few days previous with West India fruit, and by the cunning and duplicity of the Yankee skipper and his crew, many slaves in the neighborhood were induced to go on board. As soon as a load of the deluded creatures was obtained, the vessel drifted off, and setting all sail, despite the tears and entreaties of the negroes, who too late discovered the trap in which they were caught, bore them off as prizes no doubt to Yankee cupidity and love of gain. If anybody believes that some of these slaves will be resold into bondage, he has more faith in their professed philanthropy than their past history and recent actions justify.

Richmond Dispatch, June ...

A JOYFUL RETURN.

Joe, a servant of a gentleman of this city, who has been an absentee from his master's premises about eighteen months, and during that time employed by the Abolitionists on St. Helena and the adjacent islands, returned on Friday morning to his master. He reports the negroes on the island in a destitute condition, and many anxious to return had they the facilities for doing so. He is very much emaciated, but will soon recover under home influences.—*Charleston Courier.*

THE RETURN OF A SLAVE.

A negro, named Jesse, the property of R. B. Kimball, of this city, who, it will be remembered, made his escape from this port in July or August last, in company with four others—one of them named Abram, and belonging to Dr. S. Woff—returned this morning, perfectly disgusted with the Abolitionists. He states that when he and his companions left Mobile, they got on board the Federal steamer Pocahontas, then lying in the fleet in front of our harbor. Since then he has been in Baltimore, Washington and other Yankee cities, and says that he has found out all he wants to know about the Yankees. He says that he never was so badly treated in his life as he was on board that steamer. One half the time he had not enough to eat, and was only half-clothed, and the way they punished was awful—that they would put him in double irons and steam him, and so it was with both white and black. The negroes in the Northern cities were a most miserable and sorry set of fellows. One of those that went away with him was killed on the Mississippi River in one of the engagements there, and the others have been trying to escape for a long time, and he knows that they would give anything in the world if they could get home.

The way he got away is thus told: Last week the Pocahontas returned to Pensacola, after her cruise North, and the day after her arrival at the Navy Yard, three of the officers started out hunting and took him along to carry the game. When out, he watched his opportunity and skeedaddled; making his way through the woods until he got to the Perdido River. There he found a skiff and came over home.

Jesse gives a deplorable account of the Abolitionists, and says that all "dem dat wants to go dar may do it, but he neber is gwine to leave his master and home again." He declares that he is perfectly willing to "live and die in Dixie Land."

Mobile Tribune, February 5, 1863.

NEVER GIVE UP.

Never give up! it is wiser and better
Always to hope than once to despair;
Fling off the load of doubt's cankering fetter,

And break the dark spell of tyrannical care,
Never give up or the burden may sink you—
 Providence has kindly mingled the cup;
And in all trials or troubles, bethink you,
 The watchword of life must be, never give up.

Never give up! there are chances and changes
 Helping the hopeful a hundred to one,
And, through the dark chaos, High Wisdom arranges,
 Ever success—if you'll only hope on;
Never give up! for the wisest is boldest,
 Knowing that Providence mingles the cup,
And of all maxims the best as the oldest,
 Is the true watchword, never give up.

Never give up! though the grape shot may rattle,
 Or the full thunder cloud over you burst,
Stand like a rock, and the storm of the battle,
 Little shall harm you, although doing their worst,
Never give up! if adversity presses,
 Providence wisely has mingled the cup,
And the best counsel in all your distresses,
 Is the stout hearted watchword of never give up!

Exchange.

DR. NORTH'S TREATMENT IN A YANKEE PRISON—A FAITHFUL NEGRO—CAMP NEAR FREDERICKSBURG, FEBRUARY 8, 1863.

Dr. North, of Georgia, has just joined Anderson's Georgia Brigade, as Assistant Surgeon. This gentleman has just returned from a compulsory visit to Washington, he having been captured at Warrenton, Virginia. He was carried to the Capital prison, together with a negro boy belonging to him. On their arrival in the presence of the brute Wood, keeper of the prison, the negro was informed by the scoundrel that he was free, and could do whatever he wished. He was his own man.

The negro positively refused to quit his master and continued his refusal until exasperated, the brute ordered Dr. North to make his negro quit him. On Dr. North's refusal, he and his boy were placed in a dark dungeon and kept there for near twenty four hours. Wood expressed with many oaths his determination to keep them there for a month, but desisted when our captive officers threatened that when they arrived in Richmond they would lay this matter before President Davis, and have the *lex talionis* applied. The boy clung to his master's skirts and came back to Dixie well satisfied with having escaped the clutches of the Abolitionists. I mention this incident as it is not without its lesson.

Correspondence of the Atlanta Confederacy.

YANKEE HYPOCRISY AND BARBARITY ILLUSTRATED.

A correspondent writing from Fayette Court House, Alabama, under date of January 27, sends the following account of the barbarous treatment of two negro boys, belonging to Mr. Nance, of Pickens County, Alabama. The facts are vouched for by Dr. Shelton, of Fayette Court House:

"A company of volunteers having left Pickens County for the field of action, Mr. Nance sent two negro boys along to aid the company. Their imaginations became dazzled with the visions of Elysian fields in Yankeedom, and they went to find them. But Paradise was nowhere there, and they again sighed for home. The Yanks, however, detained them, and cut off their ears close to their heads. These negroes finally made their escape, and are now at home, with Mr. Nance, in Pickens. They are violent haters of Yankees, and their adventures and experience are a terror to negroes of that region, who learn a lesson from their brethren whose ears are left in Lincolndom.."

CONFEDERATE MONEY—ITS FUNDABILITY AND CURRENT VALUE AFTER THE FIRST LIMITED TIME FOR FUNDING MADE INTELLIGIBLE TO ALL.

No more grievous injury can possibly be inflicted upon this country than the systematic attempts made in some quarters to discredit the issues of Treasury Notes, or any part of them. The motives are various, but the great end sought to be attained is always speculation—speculation upon the ignorant fears of the people. Finance is a subject not easily mastered, and thus there is room and opportunity for scattering about fears and suspicions. The methods of procedure adapted to depreciate our currency are various also, but the most efficacious of them is the ill-boding hint and whisper of "repudiation." It is even insisted that the principle of repudiation is already adopted by our Government in limiting the time for funding Treasury Notes in eight per cent. bonds, afterwards limiting a time for funding at seven per cent., and so on.

We think it highly mischievous to allege that this means repudiation, either in whole or in part. In fact it is the agency which will prevent all necessity or excuse for repudiation, inasmuch as the funding, thus encouraged and hurried, helps to prevent the purchasing power of our remaining notes from going down to zero; and keeps the liabilities of the country within the limits of possible payment.

Besides, this constant operation of speculators in frightening people out of their notes, has an evil political effect, as well as a ruinous financial one. Every one ought to know, and lay to heart the fact, that if we establish our independence, all the Treasury Notes are as good as minted gold. To be subdued will never pay; and with this conviction—with all to win, or all to lose, in pocket as well as in honor—men will be more zealous to win the cause, or die. Life, indeed, would be a small matter to save out of the general ruin; because it would be the life of beggars as well as of slaves.

Therefore, it is distinctly disloyal to seek to discredit our currency, by scattering abroad doubts and fears. The Government and the Congress, we believe, have acted wisely in stimulating the funding of notes and diminishing (after ample notice) the too exorbitant interest on their bonds. We find some appropriate remarks on this subject in the Augusta "Constitutionalist," which present the case in a light intelligible to all.

"Let us look into the matter a little. By the act of August last Treasury Notes were fundable till 1st April in eight per cent. bonds—after that in seven per cents. But by the act of April, Treasury Notes issued prior to 1st December, except the two-year notes, were fundable till 22d of April in eight per cent. bonds—afterwards, till August next in seven per cents, after 1st August they are no longer fundable, but they are receivable, till paid, for all Government dues, except export duties, and payable, in gold or its equivalent, six months after peace. All the two-year notes are fundable till 31st July in eight per cent. bonds, payable in two years—after the 31st of July they are not fundable, but payable only when presented, and receivable for duties and taxes. All notes issued from 1st December to 6th April are fundable in seven per cent. bonds till 1st August—afterwards in four per cents, only, but receivable for duties and taxes, and payable after peace. Notes issued after 6th April are fundable in six per cents for twelve months from the first day of the month of their issue, afterwards in four per cents. This is the system adopted by the last Congress.

"We do not know how many Treasury Notes were issued previous to the 1st December, nor how many have since been funded. We estimate, however, that the issue then outstanding, exclusive of interest notes, two-year notes and one and two dollar notes, (not fundable,) was about two hundred and fifty millions. Probably seventy-five millions were funded to the 22d April, and it is hoped that the amount in all may reach 100,000,000 by August. If so, the amount of those left will be only fifty millions, every dollar of which is as good as gold for taxes, and will be absorbed under the tax bill. So that there is not the slightest reason why speculators and banks should refuse to receive notes issued prior to December—thus discrediting the currency of the country—the issues of the Confederate Treasury. Those notes are just as good as any Treasury issues, and parties refusing to receive them know it. They are always receivable for taxes, and payable six months after peace. The notes issued after 1st of December and previous to 6th April are equally good—and they are fundable after 1st August, though only in four per cents—just as all other Treasury Notes, issued after 6th April, are fundable only in four per cents, twelve months after issue. It is therefore only a ruse of interested parties, this attempt to discredit Treasury Notes, which are as good as any issues."

GOOD PROSPECTS—FINANCIAL AND COMMERCIAL.

RICHMOND, June 16, 1863.

The Richmond banks are receiving "a scoring" from the press of this and other States, for refusing to receive or pay out, hereafter, the Confederate Treasury Notes which cease to be fundable on the 1st of August. Whilst we have not approved of the proceeding, we have not lost sight of the fact that it is the policy of the Government, as indicated by the recommendation of the Secretary of the Treasury and by the action of Congress, to "demonetize" these notes as far as practicable on and after the 1st of August, and that the banks have either to refuse to circulate them now, or to continue to receive them until the date mentioned, when it is possible that they would have large amounts thrown upon their hands which they could not use, unless they and the people, by common consent, would continue to receive and pay them up as heretofore. If this be done, the funding act is, practically, nullified, and the relief expected from the retirement of a large amount of paper money defeated.

It is evident, therefore, that the bank directors had to dispose of a "dilemma." On the one hand, they would, to some extent, frustrate the purpose of Congress. On the other, they would excite distrust among certain classes of people, and, perhaps, produce a *quasi* panic. They threw the weight of their own self-interest into the balance, and, of course, decided that they would trust to the good sense and patriotism of the people to avert the probable consequence of their action.

We employed every argument to convince Congress of the impolicy of the "demonetising" system, which found favor with its leading members, and pointed out some of the evils of that system which have already presented themselves, but our counsels did not, of course, prevail, and we now have a system of finance which, in part, contemplates the forcing out of circulation, on the 1st of August, by funding and payment of taxes, of about $140,000,000 of currency. If this object is attained, the result will be highly beneficial. The currency will be depleted, and, consequently, the prices will decline, or, the notes remaining in circulation, will have an increased purchasing power. Will this be accomplished? Certainly, it will, if the action of the Richmond banks be followed up by the banks elsewhere in the Confederacy, and by the refusal of the people generally to receive the discredited notes. But, it may be accomplished without this wholesale discrediting, and hence we are disposed to believe that the banks were too precipitate in ruling out the old issue.

The theory of the Treasury Department is that the process of funding and the tax levy will absorb all, or the greater portion of this issue. This expectation is so reasonable that we have heretofore expressed the earnest hope that the merchants, tradesmen and others should continue to receive, at least, a portion of the notes issued prior to December 1st. For the same reason, we believe that the banks could have postponed their action until the middle of July, by which time it is possible that the very "slow coach"—the "War Tax," will begin to make itself felt as an absorbent of redundant cash. The banks adhered to their resolution, and the business men, instead of conferring together, and acting in concert, are rejecting or receiving the old issue, according to their individual avarice, patriotism, or views of inexpediency.

It is obvious that much needless vexation, inconvenience, distrust and loss will result from even the partial exclusion of these notes from circulation. If every man would receive, say one-half or one-fourth of them in the payment of a debt, they would be kept afloat until the war tax collector presented his bills, and then, as everybody, with a grain of sense, would pay his taxes in these notes, they would, of course, gradually disappear from circulation, and the object of the funding act be accomplished. We trust, therefore, that the people generally will continue to circulate them as freely as they did unbankable North Carolina notes, before the war. Those who refuse to do so will subject themselves to a disparaging remembrance.

Mr. J. S. O'Sullivan, of New York, late Minister of the United States to Portugal, has written a lengthy and eloquent letter in favor of "peace at all hazards." His letter is dated at London, 13th April, 1863, and contains this declaration:

"As a trustee, I would at this moment prefer to place trust funds for permanent investment in the Southern war debt, at par, rather than in the Northern at one-fourth of its face. The one can be paid and will be paid; the other neither will nor can."

In this declaration we have the judgment of an intelligent and unprejudiced observer of the war in this country. He views the contest from a stand-point which enables him to form a correct opinion of the probable result, and in exercising his reasoning faculties, he has evidently been aided by a just comprehension of the resources of the States composing the Confederacy. The confidence he expresses in the redemption of our war debt is shared by those capitalists of Great Britain who have subscribed to the Confederate loan recently effected in London, and we doubt not the judgment upon which this confidence is based prevails in every intelligent and unbiased circle in Europe.

If this be so, (and who can gainsay it?) might not a much stronger degree of confidence in the ability of the Confederate Government to meet and liquidate every pecuniary obligation exist among the people of the Confederate States? We are happy to know it does exist, to a very wide extent, but at the same time, there is too much tenacity on the part of gold-hoarders, who constitute a very large amount of specie. This tenacious grasp of the precious gold cannot be construed otherwise than as a distrust of the result of the contest. If we are to achieve our independence, why hold on to gold coin, which brings in no interest whilst Confederate Bonds are so easily purchased, which do yield interest? We do not argue that it is neither patriotic nor wise to hold any gold, but we would ask those who have put away coin to consider whether the time has not now arrived when they should part with at least a portion of their hoards? Gold is wanted for commercial purposes, and there may be persons who have become glutted with gain who are eager to convert their Treasury Notes into specie. The demand certainly exists, and this, together with the scarcity, has put the premium up to a high figure. The brokers will give about $15 in Treasury Notes for $2 in gold. Is this not allurement enough, if it be true, as Mr. O'Sullivan says, that the Confederate war debt "can and will be paid?" But we will not pursue the subject. Every one must determine for himself whether he will be wise or foolish in holding on to his gold when he can sell it for $7 premium, and invest the money in seven per cent. Confederate Bonds at par. We are on the eve of important and decisive events, and people may well be excused for awaiting the issue of those events, but the developement may be attended with a collapse in the premium for specie, and thus the "golden opportunity" alluded to may be lost.

Confederate eight per cent. bonds were sold at auction in Augusta, Ga., on the 12th inst., at $125, and interest. We presume they were registered bonds of the fifteen million loan.

Richmond Whig.

INDEX

	PAGE
A Female Soldier	7
A Female Aid-de-Camp	7
Miss Belle Boyd, "The Rebel Spy."	8
Miss Norah McCartey—A Reminiscence of the Missouri Campaign	9
A Brave Girl	12
Fiendish Outrage upon Women	12
Unparalleled Atrocity of Yankee Demons	13
The Women of Winchester, Va.	14
A Spirited Lady of North Carolina	14
Murdering Women	15
The Bayonet! The Needle! The Plow!	15
A Patriotic Lady	16
Patriotic Contribution	16
Yankees or Hyenas?	16
The Virtues of woman	17
What can Woman do?	19
"God's Last, Best Gift to Man," Woman a Ministering Angel	21
Beautiful Eulogium and Tribute to Woman—Woman's Heroism	22
The Society of Woman	22
To all Southern Ladies	23
Why not Import Provisions?	24
Atrocities of the Federals	25
Yankee Brutality	26
An Appeal from Women	26
Bitter Female Secessionists	28
An Artful Dodge	29
Acts of Kindness and Devotion of the Ladies of Louisville, Ky.	29
Mourn thou Land of Flowers—Banishment of Families from St. Augustine, Florida—Inhuman Treatment of Women and Children—The Federals at N. Orleans, Louisiana	30
A Cry for Vengeance—Later from Missouri	32
Home for Invalid Ladies—Interesting Correspondence—Woman Always Foremost in Promoting a Good Cause—God Bless Her Efforts with Success	34
The Worth of Woman	39
Man and Woman	40
The Women of the West	40
Atrocities of Lincoln's Officials	41
The Ladies Making Shoes	41
The Ladies and Gen. Price—Presentation to Gen. Price	41
The Greatest Atrocity yet of the Enemy	48
Robbery of a Lady	44
Patriotic and True Devotion of Woman	44
Startling Revelations by a Missourian who was to have been Hung by the Yankees	46
The Ten Missouri Murders	46
Atrocious Murder by Yankees in Missouri	47
Incidents of the Battle of Fredericksburg—The People of the Town who Remained—The Women	49
A Confederate Alphabet	50
Northern Virtue	51
Union Sentiment in New Orleans	51
The Greatest Battle	52
Gen. Lee's Address to his Army	52
First Naval Victory in Virginia—History of the Merrimac and her Commander, Admiral Franklin Buchanan	53
The First Naval Victory on the Mississippi River by Gen. Jeff. Thompson	57
Official Report of the Naval Engagement and Victory at Galveston, Texas	60
Interesting Order of Maj. Gen. Magruder—Complimentary Acknowledgment of the daring and gallantry of officers and men who vied with each other in the great Naval Engagement with the Blockading Fleet on the Coast of Texas	61

is based prevails in every intelli-
Europe.
If this be so, (and who in her
stronger degree of confiden ... 63
Government to meet and press
exist among the people ye wit-
happy to know it d ory — Yankee
same time, ! Repulsed with Great
Vigor — loss....................... 71
A Yankee Estimate of General
  Beauregard................... 74
The Fight at Charleston........ 75
Wailing and gnashing of teeth by
  the Yankees—The last hours
  of the Keokuk............... 76
A wail from the "Tribune."..... 76
Charleston Impregnable........ 77
Interesting History of the Open-
  ing of the Alabama's Career... 77
Confederate Steamer Alabama—
  The London "Times" on the
  "290."....................... 81
Confederate Steamer Alabama... 81
The Sea Fight between the Hat-
  teras and the Alabama........ 82
The Steamer Alabama at King-
  ston—A Curious Incident of
  the War..................... 83
An Incident connected with the
  sailing and running of the
  Blockade by the Confederate
  war steamer Florida.......... 83
The Terrors of the Sea—Career
  of the Florida—Description of
  her officers and style........ 84
The Confederate war steamer
  Florida at Barbadoes......... 86
The Retribution................ 86
A compliment to Liverpool..... 87
A Rattlesnake on the Ocean.... 87
Progress of the War—Affecting
  Incident—One of the results of
  the War..................... 88
Incidents of the capture of the
  Harriet Lane................. 89
Queen of the West—Further Par-
  ticulars..................... 89
The capture of the United States
  gunboat Indianola on the Mis-
  sissippi—Enemies Account.... 91
Ships against Forts............ 91
The Battle at Genesis Point.... 93
Interesting sketch of Ingraham
  and Rutledge................. 93

United States and Confeder-
  ate Naval Forces............. 96
A duty paramount to every con-
  sideration of profit—An appeal
  to raise Breadstuffs......... 99
The appeal of the Alabama Dele-
  gation....................... 101
Planting and Farming Hints.... 102
Spare the Gardens............. 103
Home Medicines—The Poppy for
  Opium........................ 103
"Farming in the South"........ 103
The Cheapest Food............. 104
Something to be Done.......... 104
A Model Boy................... 104
Gen. Pillow and the President... 105
Stampede of Contraband Troops. 105
A valuable suggestion to Plant-
  ers.......................... 106
Patriotism of Negroes—The old
  Drummer of Chalmette........ 106
Negro Patriotism.............. 106
A Loyal Negro................. 107
The Murder of the Black Race.. 108
No Love for Sambo—Negroes ex-
  pelled from Indiana.......... 109
The Negroes to be forced to fight. 110
One Yankee and three Negroes
  Buried in one Hole........... 110
The Negroes begin to "Hurt" in
  Massachusetts................ 110
A full Yankee Lieutenant a Ne-
  gro.......................... 111
The Negro in this War......... 111
Crime and its Punishment...... 112
The Key to the Prosperity of the
  Confederacy.................. 112
The Negro and the Yankee—The
  Yankee Hangs the Negro—and
  his opinion of him........... 112
Derivation and Meaning of the
  word Yankee.................. 113
New Slave Trade............... 113
A Joyful Return............... 114
The Return of a Slave......... 114
Never Give Up................. 114
Dr. North's Treatment in a Yan-
  kee Prison—A Faithful Ne-
  gro—Camp near Fredericks-
  burg, February 8, 1863....... 115
Yankee Hypocrisy and Barbari-
  ty Illustrated............... 116
Confederate Money—Its Funda-
  bility and Current Value after
  the first limited time for Fund-
  ing made Intelligible to all.. 116
Good Prospects—Financial and
  Commercial................... 118

www.ingramcontent.com/pod-product-compliance
Lightning Source LLC
Chambersburg PA
CBHW022141160426
43197CB00009B/1386